The Beginner's Guide to Wealth

To the Young People of the World: Our Future
Depends on You.

Noel Whittaker
James Whittaker

16

EasyRead Large

Copyright Page from the Original Book

Other bestsellers by Noel Whittaker:
MAKING MONEY MADE SIMPLE
MORE MONEY WITH NOEL WHITTAKER
LIVING WELL IN RETIREMENT
GOLDEN RULES OF WEALTH
CONTROLLING YOUR CREDIT CARDS
SUPERANNUATION MADE SIMPLE
SHARES MADE SIMPLE
LOANS MADE SIMPLE
DRIVING SMALL BUSINESS
MONEY TIPS
SUPERANNUATION MADE EASY
25 ESSENTIAL SITES FOR MASTERING YOUR MONEY
25 ESSENTIAL SITES FOR MASTERING SMALL BUSINESS
25 ESSENTIAL SITES FOR MASTERING YOUR LIFE
SAVING TAX ON YOUR INVESTMENT PROPERTY

THE BEGINNER'S GUIDE TO WEALTH
First published in Australia in 2010 by
Simon & Schuster (Australia) Pty Limited
Suite 2, Lower Ground Floor, 14–16 Suakin Street, Pymble NSW 2073

A CBS Company
Sydney New York London Toronto

Visit our website at www.simonandschuster.com.au

National Library of Australia
Cataloguing-in-Publication data:

Whittaker, Noel, 1940– .
The beginner's guide to wealth / Noel Whittaker, James Whittaker.

Includes index.
ISBN 9780731813612 (pbk)

Subjects: Finance, Personal.
Financial security.
Young adults—Finance, Personal.

Other Authors/Contributors: Whittaker, James Patrick 1983– .

332.024

Cover design by Sharon Felschow
Cartoons by Paul Lennon
Typeset in Australia by dta studio, Brendale, Queensland, 4500
Printed in Australia by Griffin Press

10 9 8 7 6 5 4 3 2 1

ReadHowYouWant partners with publishers to provide books for ALL Kinds of Readers. For more information about Becoming A **RHYW** Registered Reader and to find more titles in your preferred format, visit:
www.readhowyouwant.com

TABLE OF CONTENTS

ABOUT THE AUTHORS

Noel Whittaker is one of Australia's best known financial advisers and is a founding director of Whittaker Macnaught Pty Ltd, a leading financial planning organisation.

He is a pioneer in the field of consumer education and his books *Making Money Made Simple* and *More Money with Noel Whittaker* are international best-sellers. He writes weekly columns in many major Australian newspapers including the *Sydney Morning Herald,* Brisbane *Sunday Mail,* Perth *Sunday Times* and the Brisbane *Courier-Mail.* He also appears regularly on radio and television, is in demand as a motivational speaker and has addressed large audiences in Australia and overseas.

His services to the financial planning industry were recognised in 1988 when he received the award of Australian Investment Planner of the Year.

He is married with three children and his hobbies are gardening and golf. His special interest is studying what makes people happy.

Noel has used his experiences to form much of the content of this book, working with his son James to shape the book you are now reading.

James Whittaker is the Business Development Manager for Whittaker Macnaught, where he has worked since 2003. James has completed a Bachelor of Business Management (majoring in Marketing and Real Estate & Development) and a Bachelor of Arts (majoring in English and Writing) from the University of Queensland. He has also completed a Diploma of Financial Services (Financial Planning) through Kaplan.

James is passionate about personal development and enjoys studying human potential. For many years he has provided valuable feedback to Noel regarding the content of articles and books that Noel has written.

ACKNOWLEDGEMENTS

When you write a book you appreciate the value of teamwork. *The Beginners Guide to Wealth* has developed from a combination of the efforts of a large group of talented and enthusiastic people who unstintingly gave of their time to help put the book in your hand.

A special thank you is due to Noel's wife Geraldine for the hours she spent debating the content of each chapter. To Helen Birch for the editing, Sharon Felschow for cover design, Paul Lennon for the cartoons and Brenda Partridge and Kira McNeill for reading the proofs and making valuable suggestions.

INTRODUCTION

Since its release in 1987 *Making Money Made Simple* has become recognised as the standard work for people who wish to learn the principles of saving and investing money. Seldom a day passes that I don't receive at least one letter or email telling me how that book has changed somebody's life.

I became used to comments of "Why don't they teach this in schools?" or "I wish I had read this when I was young" but gradually I began to realise that young people had a special need—a book written especially for them to show them where to start. After all, you have to learn to make money before you can manage it.

The resolve to write such a book strengthened when I was at a 21st birthday party for the daughter of a friend. During the evening I started chatting with a group of bright young people—the kind of men and women you would expect to be our future leaders. To my amazement they feared the future, were scared at the prospect of trying to find a job and were concerned about their ability to handle the challenges that life will undoubtedly present to them. I left thinking "If these people feel like this, what must the others be going through?"

Soon afterwards, in unrelated incidents, two couples who were clients of our company suffered the trauma of having a teenage child commit suicide.

There was no warning or obvious reason, in either case.

A teenage suicide is a tragic waste of an important life and these incidents reinforced my belief that many of our young people are experiencing feelings of confusion and inadequacy as they try to cope with the challenges of a new era dominated by technology and a drive for efficiency at all costs. While these feelings are understandable, it is true that every generation has had its difficulties and the techniques for personal growth and achievement that have worked before will continue to work now.

The aim of this book is to show you how to approach the challenges that lie ahead and to guide you into a success pattern instead of a failure pattern. The way to success is getting harder, but those who are prepared will find there are boundless opportunities waiting to be taken. As the great inventor Thomas Edison said, "If we did all the things we are capable of doing we would literally astound ourselves". The recipe for wealth is quite simple: you just need to be earning more than you are spending so you have money left over to invest. Once you can do that, it's only a matter of investing the surplus wisely. This book will show you how to improve your skills to increase your income and then explain simple strategies to make your money work for you.

I am delighted that my son James has joined Whittaker Macnaught and am thrilled that he has consented to co-author this book with me. He brings a young person's insight to the book that I could not achieve on my own.

Our wish for you is that you will approach the future with confidence instead of fear and that you will astound yourself at what you find you can do. The future of our world depends on it.

NOEL WHITTAKER

1

PUT ON YOUR RUNNING SHOES

You only pass through this life once; you don't come back for an encore.

Elvis Presley

Young people in the 21st century face a radically different world from the one in which their parents grew up. The remarkable technological advances in the last 50 years coupled with changes in social attitudes have given many people vastly improved living standards. Nowadays we use the internet or television to watch events as they happen around the world. Computers have taken much of the drudgery out of office work, miracle drugs have improved our life expectancy, heavy machinery has replaced backbreaking work, and discrimination because of sex or race is becoming less common.

However, every action has an opposite reaction. Because computers and robots are doing a larger share of the routine jobs, we achieve a higher output with fewer staff. People are living longer because of medical breakthroughs and improved health care facilities but this all needs funding. As job availability shrinks and more people join the unemployment queues, those taxpayers left in the workforce have to provide funds for a larger welfare bill. Fortunately, Australia has enjoyed a low unemployment rate in the last few years, but the real test will be whether this is sustainable.

The world is rapidly being transformed from an industrial economy to an information-driven economy. Production, administrative and clerical jobs will become scarce as the transformation continues. To make matters worse, our major businesses will not hesitate to outsource their operations if conditions are more favourable somewhere else in the world.

For business managers now, the buzz words are "efficiency, productivity and customer focus". In simple language, that says they want to look after their customers better but use fewer staff to do it. This means there will be fewer jobs available and more people trying to get them. The bad news is that it's getting tougher out there; the good news is that there's an abundance of outstanding opportunities everywhere for those who are ready.

To take advantage of the opportunities that lie ahead, you will have to learn how to make the right choices in your life. You can choose to handle the future in one of two ways:

(1)   Complain about how unfair things have become, give up trying, and despair of ever getting anywhere in such a difficult and changing world.

   or

(2)   Take the situation as a challenge and make the best of it.

Certainly the world is changing and you face a different set of problems from those your parents and grandparents had to cope with. But remember they also had problems—they just differed from yours. Epictetus, a Greek slave who became a very respected and influential philosopher, famously said, "It's not what happens to you, but how you react to it that matters."

As we start you on your journey to success, you need to be aware that people have always faced challenges and that you are lucky to be living where you are now. Imagine if you lived in an overcrowded Third World country, or had been born to poor parents 200 years ago and were working in a mine or a factory at the age of nine.

While every age has, and will have, its own challenges, there is another factor that you must accept. There have always been some who used the challenges as springboards to success. To do this they adopted some simple, universal and timeless principles that we will teach you in the chapters that follow.

We promise you these principles are **not** hard to understand and they will lead you to a successful life. All you have to do is follow them. That may sound a promise from Hogwarts but it will happen. You can be among the few lucky ones because most people never learn these principles and, many of those who do, never make the effort to put them into practice.

As you read you will come across names like Napoleon Hill, Og Mandino, W. Clement Stone, Denis Waitley, Samuel Smiles, Wayne Dyer and Jim Rohn. These are men whose writings have inspired the world. There is more information about them at the back of the book.

Now might be an appropriate time for a story. It sounds at first like just a joke but it has a message that's really worth thinking about.

Two people were hiking through the jungle when they heard the sound of a tiger nearby. Both were terrified but one stopped and started to put on a pair of running shoes. "What do you think you are doing?" said the other. "You know you can't outrun a tiger no matter what you are wearing on your feet."

"I don't have to outrun the tiger," was the response. "I only have to beat you!"

That's the way the world is going. The gap between the "haves" and the "have nots" will widen as jobs become harder to get and the work available splits further into skilled and unskilled. You can put on your running shoes safe in the knowledge that over 80% of the population will worry about what is happening yet will do nothing to improve their situation. It is the minority who will take action, such as reading this book, and change their lives for the better.

As this book is probably your introduction to the subject of success, we have tried to make it an easy read for you. Most of the chapters are short and every one has one major message that is repeated continually to stamp it on your mind. At the end of each chapter you will have to decide if you want to keep on going or "tap out". It's a bit like the TV game show where the player has the choice of taking the money now or coming back next week to win more. There is just one difference with this book—the chapters don't get any harder. If you can follow one you can follow the next.

Make your first choice now. If you are not interested in improving your life, stop here and give the book to somebody else. However, if you want to make the most of the potential you have, and the tremendous opportunities you have been given, put on your running shoes and read on.

The vault:

- Take each situation as a challenge and make the best of it.
- It's not what happens to you but how you react to it that matters.

– Increase your skills to become one of the "haves".
– Put on your running shoes!

2

IT'S NOT AN ACCIDENT

Action may not always bring happiness, but there is no happiness without action.

Benjamin Disraeli

The message of this chapter is that success in life is a decision, not an accident of birth or a lucky break. Your future depends on the actions you take from now on. What you have done in the past is of no importance.

You are holding this book in your hands because:
(1)   Somebody gave it to you
or
(2)   You bought it for yourself.

If somebody gave it to you, they must have thought that reading the book would give you some clues to a happier life. Congratulate yourself for being fortunate enough to know somebody who believes in you. That's a great advantage.

If you bought it for yourself, deep down you probably feel the itch of frustration—a feeling that life is like a beautiful valley waiting for you once you cross the mountain. The problem is that the mountain looks forbidding and there are many well-worn trails at the bottom of it. You've tried a few that didn't take you anywhere and you're reaching a stage where you're scared to try many more in case you discover that none of them will take you anywhere either. That's how so many of us feel. You could sum it up by saying you've got a feeling you could really be something if only you knew where to begin.

Read on. This book will start you on the right path and help you unlock some of that potential stored inside you. Congratulate yourself for being courageous enough to start taking charge of your future.

LIVING ON BISCUITS

We'll start with a story about an elderly couple:

They had lived a thrifty life but decided to have a final fling with part of the retirement cheque when the husband finished work. They booked a 14-day boat cruise but spent so much money on the tickets that there was little left over for spending money. To overcome the problem, and to keep their spare money for shopping, they worked out a plan to save money on meals. They bought a large tin of biscuits and, instead of dining in the ship's restaurant, ate biscuits for breakfast, lunch and dinner in their cabin.

They got very tired of living on biscuits, but the weather was great, the company was fine, and they had the best holiday of their life. On the final night of the cruise they carefully counted up how much spending money remained and decided they could afford to break out and eat their final dinner in the ship's dining room.

They got all dressed up and prepared for a memorable evening. However, when they arrived at the plush dining room they were puzzled when the head waiter escorted them to a superb table and handed them the huge menus because there were no prices shown. When they asked why, the waiter replied, "Of course there are no prices—the meals are included in the cost of the fare!"

They had spent the whole trip eating biscuits because they had not realised the meals were included. What a waste!

Life is like that. Most people go through life living on the equivalent of biscuits because they never knew how much else was available. A fortunate few learn the lesson when they are young—as we hope you will—and some, like Noel, do not learn it until they are 35. The majority never learn it at all.

James says...

Humans, as a whole, have undergone more changes in the last century than we have in all previous centuries since the dawn of time. We are becoming a society reliant on coffee and junk food, wasting away in front of computers and the latest gaming consoles, and sourcing pleasure from areas that don't always assist in our personal growth and development.

Sure, these things can be fun—in moderation—but anymore than that and it becomes a negative routine that can be difficult to break out of. It's so easy to fall into this routine, and that's why so many of us do it.

These habits, as well as our evolutionary hardwiring, have also created a more anxious society, as the gap between what we did thousands of years ago is replaced by modern living.

It is so easy to live a mediocre life, and that's why so many of us do it. Prioritise your hours and then reflect—do you have potential that's going to waste?

SUCCESS IS FOR YOU

The message of this chapter is that success is available for you—if you know how to achieve it. Right now you may be thinking "It's all right for somebody like Noel to talk about success, he has never experienced the problems I have".

Noel says...

Let me tell you a little about my background. I was born in 1940 just as World War II was breaking out. My father managed a pig farm and I went to a small country school. In 1954 the farm was sold and we found ourselves with no home because we had always lived on the farm in the manager's house. My father was out of a job and the only place he could find work was as a labourer in a foundry.

I was so clumsy at school that the manual arts teacher would hold up my pathetic efforts at woodwork for all the class to laugh at. I was dropped from most of the health and physical education classes and never made a sporting team. When I finished high school I decided I was too dumb to go to university and, instead, joined the Bank of New South Wales (now Westpac) because it was a long-established institution and I wanted a safe job. For the first 35 years of my life I suffered with a massive inferiority complex and did not start to realise my potential until I read Think and Grow Rich *by Napoleon Hill. My life was transformed from that moment.*

The main reason I wrote Making Money Made Simple *was to save people all those years*

I wasted. The reason for writing the book you are now holding was to get a similar message across to people but in a way that is specially tailored to the young so they can put the principles into practice sooner.

You **must** understand that success in life is not dependent on what your background is, what has happened to you in the past, how brainy you are, how good looking you are or how much luck comes your way. Sure, some people do seem to get a great start in life because of some special talent or circumstances but for the rest of us **there is always a compensating factor.** In fact, many gifted people find everything all too easy at first and never learn the important habits of persistence and patience. Having wealthy parents can be more of a hindrance than a help. Children of the so-called "wealthy and glamorous" movie stars or members of the royal family have certainly had their fair share of problems, and made worse because they're often made very public (as you can see by picking up a newspaper or reading the latest news website).

Many young people from poor backgrounds discover that their early experiences provides the spur for them to do better than their parents. They may not have done as well in life if they had come from privileged backgrounds. Others learned from a tough background. Comedian Billy Connolly, talk show host Oprah Winfrey, rugby league coach Wayne Bennett and author J.K. Rowling are just a few who endured significant personal hardship at a young age before fighting their way to the pinnacle of their chosen field. And some of the most prominent figures through history, such as Winston Churchill, Albert Schweitzer, Gandhi, Albert Einstein and Sigmund Freud, battled against adversity until they achieved their goals. Often the drive to compensate for a disadvantage (whether it be a physical handicap, poverty, parental abuse or any number of other things) can drive people to remarkable journeys of personal achievement.

Studies show that only a small number of family businesses survive to the third generation.[1] The process goes like this:

(1) The grandparents start to build a business from scratch. They pick up the necessary skills along the way and most of what they learn is from experience.

(2) The next generation learns directly from the founders and, when the founders die, take over a thriving business. However, the founders had the unique experience of building from nothing, whereas the second generation received help from their parents.

(3) The members of the third generation are born to wealth and are too often protected by their parents from the chance to learn. Because the

---

[1] Benson B, Crego E, Drucker R. Your Family Business. A Success Guide for Growth and Survival. (1990) Business One Irwin IL. USA.

grandchildren never had the chance to learn the skills of their parents and grandparents they are unable to handle the problems of the now large business and it may go into decline or be sold. The third generation often ends up broke and the cycle starts all over.

This has given rise to the expression: "Shirt sleeves to shirt sleeves in three generations".

So forget about using your background as an excuse and remember that we all have potential we can put to use. In this book I will show you that success in life is predictable and that it can almost always be achieved if you follow certain rules. Therefore there are two major steps: learn what has to be done, and then put it into practice. You can do it if **you want to.**

The vault:

- Your future depends on the actions you take from now on.
- Success is available for you—if you know how to achieve it.
- Many gifted people find everything all too easy at first and never learn the important habits of persistence and patience.
- Ignore your background—we all have potential we can put to use.
- Learn what has to be done, and then put it into practice.

3

SUCCESS—WHAT IS IT?

I want to be all that I am capable of becoming.

Katherine Mansfield

The aim of this book is to help you to become a "success". Therefore, in this chapter we'll think about what the word means.

Becoming "successful" is a bit like becoming "happy"; the words have different meanings for everybody. One dictionary defines success as "the accomplishment of an aim" and "good fortune". On his bestselling audio recording, *The Strangest Secret* (which you can find online), Earl Nightingale describes success as "the realisation of a worthy goal". You will have to find your own definition, but personally we regard successful people as those who are in control of their life, who are working at what they enjoy, and who are contributing to society.

Think of your life as travelling in a car. You can choose to be in the driver's seat, deciding where to go, how fast to go, and when to take a break. This involves planning the route, keeping a watch on the road ahead, and allowing for events such as hail storms, accidents or road blocks that may hold you up. You are also responsible for putting the fuel in

the car and paying for the repairs. You experience both the pleasure and the responsibility. You are in charge.

You can choose to be a passenger in which case you will have no say over where the car goes and you will just have to hope it travels in the direction that you want to go. There is no need to look out the window or to plan ahead. You can stay safely inside and be at the mercy of somebody else's decisions and never have any say in your life. Whether you choose to be a driver or a passenger is up to you but according to our definition, successful people are the ones who have taken control of their life and are living it on their terms. **They** are in the driver's seat.

Just be aware that it is possible to be a success in one area of your life and not in another. This is called being "out of balance". A common example is the business executive who works long hours and is probably considered highly successful at work but who neglects health and family and thus spends most of the time suffering extreme pressure. The outcome is often a physical and mental breakdown coupled with the realisation, too late, that they have missed most of the true joys of life.

Success to us is:

Working at a job you **enjoy** instead of one you hate.

Owning your **own home** so you are not at the mercy of a landlord who may force you to move out.

Having the financial freedom to **travel** and experience the wonders of our unique world.

Having **fulfilling** and happy personal relationships instead of living in conflict.

Freedom to choose. It's a great feeling to go to a shop and choose on the basis of what you want rather than what you can afford.

Feeling **good** about yourself.

Having a **well-rounded** life so you enjoy a range of activities.

We promise you that if you follow what is in this book, you will have a better life, you will be financially secure, you will wake up on most mornings looking forward to the day, you will have happy relationships and you will feel good about yourself. You will also discover some incredible powers within yourself. We are **not** promising you total freedom from problems or stress, but if you follow the principles in this book you will find they are a part of life that you will take in your stride.

GIVING UP TO GET

This is a good time to tell you about another important concept—to move forward you must give up. Saving for a home means you have to give up spending all your pay. The reward is the security of owning your own home. Having children means giving up personal freedom for the joy of being a parent. Becoming an adult involves giving up being taken care of in return for being able to make your own decisions. A fit body involves giving up some of the fun of gorging on junk food. Owning your own business means giving up the security of working for somebody else in exchange for the chance to run your own life.

Giving up is a fact of life and none of us can change it. The good news is that you will find that by giving up you can achieve more than you had before. There are great rewards.

In the next chapter you will learn your first lesson—how to avoid the negative pull of those around you.

The vault:

- Find your own definition of "success" but, generally, successful people are the ones who have taken control of their life and are living it on their terms.
- To move forward, you must be prepared to give up less important things to reach a more important goal.

4

MOST PEOPLE

We forfeit three-fourths of ourselves in order to be like other people.

Arthur Schopenhauer

The message of this chapter is that most people never learn or practise success habits and, as a result, die without using their potential. They often drift through life working at jobs they don't enjoy, dreading the thought of Mondays and, yet, fear the loss of their jobs. They usually end up living on welfare convinced that life has dealt them a cruel hand.

In *Making Money Made Simple* Noel discussed research that had been carried out on typical 16-year-olds.

By the time they are 65:
- 76% of them are either dead or dead broke
- 16% are getting by
- Only 8%—that's one in every 12—have made it financially.

That's a scary lot of figures, but what do they say to you?

It should tell you that most people are doing it wrong. Now this is an extremely valuable piece of information—if most are doing it wrong it should follow that if you do what they do, you will be on the wrong track too. Maybe it also follows that doing things **differently** may be a recipe for success.

Earl Nightingale claims "Winners do the things that failures aren't prepared to do", while Brian Tracy believes "Winners spend their time on activities that produce results, whereas losers spend their time on activities that relieve tension".

Let's think about what most people do and don't do. I can tell you one activity they **love** to do. As James said in Chapter 2, most people waste at least 20 hours a week watching television or playing video games, and they **never** read books or take courses that will improve their mind.

They also can't wait to finish their work at the end of the day, can't wait for Friday to come, never set goals, and spend their whole lives wishing they could win the lottery so they would never have to work again.

In a later chapter you will learn your rewards in life will match your service. Therefore, it should be obvious that those who spend life providing no meaningful service to anybody else will get rewards in keeping with that effort. It may also explain why so many lottery winners who were broke when they won the money are back to being broke a couple of years after the big win.

"What about peer pressure?" We hear you say. "If all my friends are having a good time, why can't I?" Hold it. We have never written anything that suggests people shouldn't have a good time.

But understand there is a time to resist peer pressure. Otherwise you will end up like the majority, which we now know is not all it's cracked up to be.

The aim of this book is to enable you to have the greatest time you could imagine by showing you ways to become more than you ever dreamed of. Be assured—the views are better from the house that overlooks the water.

THE GREAT ESCAPE

Noel was one of the guest speakers at a convention in Fiji and sat enthralled as a high earning 24 year old told his story to a large audience. He had been a shearer but found the work hard and the shearing sheds hot. His goal was to break out of those sheds to find a job he enjoyed and to make more money. He told how he would spend night after night reading books like *Think and Grow Rich* and how the other shearers, who were more concerned with drinking, teased him about it.

His reply to them was "One day I'll be out of these shearing sheds and you guys will still be stuck here." The goal of a better life kept him on track and able to withstand the pressure from his workmates who, as far as he knows, are still shearing sheep and wishing they were doing something else.

We know it can be hard to withstand pressure from your fellow human beings, but there are two solutions: you can either lead the group in the direction in which you want to travel, or you can change your circle of friends to one that has goals and dreams that fit with yours.

Example: *Mark wants to stop smoking, lose some weight and get fit. He has difficulty in getting motivated because all his friends eat junk food, smoke heavily and drink too much. However, if Mark joins the local gym he will meet people who are keen to keep fit and healthy, and will probably discover there is just as much fun in going for a run than hanging around bars and clubs.*

Alternatively he could do his friends a service and organise the whole group to go jogging three or four times a week. Deep down they would probably all welcome this, but nobody has got around to suggesting it.

We cannot stress enough the power of the people you mix with. We know that people will respond well if you take them out of their environment (work or home), give them a good course with top instructors and teach them a bunch of skills. However, the whole value of the course is generally lost within a few weeks if they return to their old environment and mix with the same negative people. The only solution is to send the whole group to the same course.

The reason for slipping back into the old pattern of behaviour is obvious when you think about it. It takes more effort to climb the mountain than to slip down it, and usually the worst course of action for you is the easiest one. It takes effort to refuse a cigarette when your friends are having one and to say, "I can't afford to go out—I am saving for a home," when everybody is planning a night on the town. It is far simpler to mix with people who have compatible goals with yours. Then you can all agree to have a cheap night out or stay at home and make your own fun.

TAPPING IN

Another way to resist peer pressure is to be part of what Napoleon Hill called a "mastermind" group. This is a group of people with similar goals who meet with the common purpose of helping one another achieve them. Hill regarded such a group as so important that he devoted the first chapter of his famous book *The Law of Success* to the idea. He states he has proved time and time again that "every human brain is both a broadcasting and a receiving station for vibrations of thought and frequency".[2]

He believed the coming together of several minds created a mind that was bigger than all the others put together.

James says...

Several years ago after hearing about the concept of a mastermind group, three friends and I decided to meet regularly and tap into our combined knowledge. We discussed business ideas and concepts, financial information and investment proposals, and nominated a person each meeting to present their ideas to the group (this allowed us to all improve our public speaking skills too). We were from fairly different disciplines, but this allowed us to learn about things we weren't so

---

2   Hill, Napoleon. The Law of Success (1929) 1979 Edition published by Success Unlimited.

familiar with, and enhance our knowledge for areas we did understand.

The group also made a commitment to put away a certain amount of money each month, which we would eventually invest in companies that we had researched ourselves.

To this day, we still catch up at least once a month for educational purposes, to discuss case studies on interesting companies and speak frankly about future business opportunities.

This is a highly rewarding avenue to explore, and I would recommend it to anyone for the knowledge it brings, all in an environment that allows you to catch up with your friends.

We don't want to spend too much time on the mastermind concept as this book is intended to be only an introduction to a new and exciting world for you. As you learn more about success you will find the concept of a mastermind group comes up regularly and, as your awareness grows, the right people will start to appear in your life. The point we want to get across is the massive power exerted on you by the people you mix with. On many occasions we've been caught up with the excitement and motivation that a determined and inspiring friendship network provides. But it's hard to avoid the pull of less focused and negative people who want to keep you from being all you can be. Make a commitment to put yourself in both of these settings, and observe the different energies that these polar opposite attitudes exude.

It happens because we tend to act like those around us. If they are negative and always blaming everybody else for their problems, they will drag you down too and you will soon start to act the same way.

Fortunately, as you practise the principles in this book, you will find that you automatically move towards people who will help you get where you want to go. There is a Buddhist saying, "When the pupil is ready the teacher will appear", and that has certainly been true for us.

The vibrations of thought that Napoleon Hill wrote about can possibly attract to us the people we need. Maybe a mind that is prepared sees opportunities that are not clear to another mind. Whatever the reason, it works.

Meanwhile don't forget that if you continue to act like the majority you will end up where they end up. Dead broke at 65!

The vault:

- If most people are doing it wrong, then doing what they do could put you on the wrong track too.
- Our rewards in life will match our service.
- You can either lead the group in the direction you want to travel or change your circle of friends to one with goals and dreams like yours.
- It takes more effort to climb the mountain than to slip down it. Usually the worst course of action is the easiest.

- A mastermind group delivers extra power to help you achieve your goals.

5

STARTING A CHAIN REACTION

It's fine to celebrate success, but it is more important to heed the lessons of failure.

Bill Gates

In this chapter you will learn how to use a magic formula to start a chain reaction that will take you where you want to go.

By now you should know that success is possible for you and understand that it **doesn't** depend on who your parents are, how brainy you are, what you look like, or what you have done so far in your life. It depends on your taking a series of steps that we'll call the "magic formula". We have used the word "magic" because of the extraordinary results that can occur once you start. Actually there is nothing magical about it at all—it's simply the laws of cause and effect operating.

Success depends on a chain reaction that you may well have already started. You take an action that leads to a further action, and then to another action, and finally you get a result that until now you may never have dreamed was possible. There is one catch:

the process often takes a long time to work, which is why many who start don't stick with it.

As Brian Tracy explained in his bestselling audio recording, *The Psychology of Success* (which can also be found online), many studies have shown that success is like baking a cake—if you use the right ingredients and mix them properly, the result is predictable. You can therefore move confidently forward secure in the knowledge that if you follow certain clearly defined steps the results will come.

You are lucky because most of the research has been done for you. Napoleon Hill spent 20 years under the guidance of the famous industrialist, Andrew Carnegie, studying the techniques used by over 100 of the most successful men and women in the world in the early 20th century. They included Henry Ford the car manufacturer, Thomas Edison the inventor, George Eastman the founder of Kodak and F. W. Woolworth who started the shopping chain.

Hill found that all these people used the magic formula and in 1927 published his findings in his book *The Law of Success.* This was such a large book that he condensed the information into his famous book *Think and Grow Rich* which has been on the bestseller lists for more than 50 years. Every time Noel makes a speech to business people he asks for a show of hands from those who have read *Think and Grow Rich.* Always a lot of hands go up and it becomes obvious that, for so many of the audience, Napoleon Hill's books were the start of their success.

Since then a multitude of books have been devoted to the subject of "success" and we have included the names of some of them in our suggested basic library (at the back of this book) because there is no doubt they have changed hundreds of thousands of lives. It is our heartfelt wish that *The Beginner's Guide to Wealth* will be at the start of your journey, which will include reading many of the other fascinating books on the subject.

Now, let's get down to work. In simple terms, the rules of achievement can be summarised as follows:

(1)　You must **believe** you have the ability.

(2)　You will have to clearly understand that you must make the effort **before** you enjoy the results.

(3)　You must set clearly defined **goals.**

(4)　You must **increase your value** as a person through continual self-development.

(5)　You must have **persistence** and **learn from your failures.**

(6)　You must maintain a **positive mental attitude.**

(7)　You must take **full responsibility** for your successes and failures.

Now we'll examine each of these factors in detail and you'll learn ways to put them all into practice. It's not difficult but it does take time and work.

As we proceed, remember that being in control is one of the ultimate achievements in life. Think about it. The winners can spend most of each day doing what they choose to do—what makes them happiest. In contrast the losers spend most of their time worrying about money and doing things they don't particularly like because they have no alternative.

The choice is yours.

BELIEVING YOU HAVE THE ABILITY

For many of you this will be the hardest part but the following techniques will help. There is more in the chapter on self-concept (Chapter 7) which shows you how your brain works, gives you methods of changing how you see yourself, and helps you think about what happened to change that unstoppable confidence with which you were born.

Look at any infant and you will see what you once were: fearless, confident, curious about everything on the planet, and with an insatiable demand for learning. No matter how often you fell over, you got up again; no matter how much the adults said, "Don't touch," you persisted. You really were a giant in the making.

Then slowly, and sadly, you began to take notice of "most people" and you started to follow the crowd. Your confidence gave way to fear and that thirst for knowledge slowly ebbed away. It became easier to conform than to be different, and much more comfortable to stagnate watching excessive television than to stretch your brain on a new skill.

The way to regain that confidence is to get it back the way you lost it—little by little. We'll go into it in detail soon.

MAKING THE EFFORT BEFORE YOU ENJOY THE RESULTS

You may think this is obvious but you'll find "most people" don't appreciate it and go through life without making any serious effort and then blaming everybody else for their failures. They have never learned that our rewards are multiplied by our output.

SETTING CLEARLY DEFINED GOALS

Ask any winner what made the difference and they will say, "Goals". Goal setting is of vital importance to success, yet it is rarely taught in schools. "Most people" have never learned how to do it. We have given it a full chapter in this book. If you follow the techniques set out in this book you will reach a stage where you will be able to achieve any realistic goal you set for yourself.

PRACTISING CONTINUALSELF-DEVELOPMENT

This is a major factor because your rewards in life are in proportion to the way you develop your skills and, as the world changes, people with the right skills will be in demand. There is a full chapter in this book on the importance of self-development but if you read between the lines you will notice the entire book is devoted to starting a process that will bring out the hidden potential that is in you now.

UNDERSTANDING FAILURE

Noel says...

One of my major problems when I was younger was that I never appreciated the effort that went into making a winner. I learned the piano for a few weeks but found it difficult and decided I had no natural ability. Then I bought a saxophone and fiddled with it for a while but never got around to serious practice. I envied the singers and musicians in the movies who could belt out a tune with no apparent effort, but got a rude awakening when I went to hear a well-known singer and orchestra and made a request for a special number. They couldn't play it because "we don't have the music for it". That was the end of my illusions about ad libbing a tune as you see happening in the movies.

It took years before I discovered that those who perform difficult feats with apparent ease have spent years of hard slog to get that way. Everything of value takes time.

Don't let the first defeat put you off trying again. To grow as a person and to develop your skills, you must stretch yourself and try things you have never done before. You would be a most extraordinary person if you could get all these new skills right the first time.

As the American writer and philosopher Elbert Hubbard said, "The greatest mistake a person can make is to be afraid of making one." There is nothing wrong with making a mistake and there is nothing wrong with failing. The only real failure is failing to try. Failure is an integral part of success and it never stopped you when you were a child learning to walk.

KEEPING A POSITIVE MENTAL ATTITUDE

If you have a positive mental attitude you expect the best from every situation. It's a strange quirk in life that we usually get what we expect; therefore it makes sense to always expect good things to happen. Luckily it is simply a habit that comes naturally after a little bit of practice.

TAKING FULL RESPONSIBILITY FOR YOUR LIFE

The main message of this book is that you can have the most wonderful life if you decide to do what is necessary to achieve it. That statement implies the actions you take from now on will determine your future. As you have the power to control these actions, it must follow that you have the power to control your future. Certainly it takes some effort but, as you will soon discover, the rewards are far greater than the effort.

The author Bryce Courtenay wrote, "It isn't hard at the top. It's easy. It isn't crowded and it's really quite civilised. What's hard is the bottom. Down there you'll find a hundred times more competition. Down there is where people stand on your teeth so that they can get a firmer foot-hold on the first rung of the ladder out of hell. Why then is it that most people seem so afraid of success that they'll do almost anything to avoid it?"[3] The choice is yours.

The vault:

- Feed your mind and develop your skills.
- Believe in yourself and your own ability.
- Winners can spend most of each day doing what they choose to do.
- Set clearly defined goals so you know where you're heading.
- Understand the value of persistence
— everything of value takes time.
- The only real failure is failing to try. Failure is an integral part of success.
- You can have the most wonderful life if you decide to do what is necessary to achieve it.

---

[3] Courtenay. Bryce. A Recipe for Dreaming (1992) William Heinemann. Australia.

6

REFRAMING: IT'S HOW YOU LOOK AT IT!

I learned that courage was not the absence of fear, but the triumph over it. The brave man is not he who does not feel afraid, but he who conquers that fear.

Nelson Mandela

The message in this chapter is that you live your life as you see it. Therefore, you can change your life by changing the way you look at it.

You have probably heard the story about two men in a bar arguing about whether a glass of beer was half full or half empty. Of course both are right; it depends on your point of view. However, even though both are right, the person who felt he still had half a glass left may have been far happier than the one who believed that his beer was nearly finished.

As you go through life you will find there are few absolutes and that what you think you see is usually **literally** what you get. Because of this, we will now explain a technique that has enormous potential to help you better your life. It is called "reframing", which means changing the way you look at something.

Understand that you can choose how you think about something. How you think may be influenced by what you have experienced before, what you think you are seeing, or how you have trained yourself to react. Here are some examples.

Noel says...

When I was a brash young 20-year-old I had just joined a golf club. One day I saw the Club President walk up to the first tee accompanied by what appeared to be a tramp. The man was dirty, scruffily dressed and, to make it worse, had trouble hitting the golf ball. The next time I saw the President I asked him why he was lowering the club standards by letting such a person on the course. His answer stunned me. "That man is a friend of mine who lost his wife and children in an accident about a year ago. His doctor thinks golf might help him." The moment I heard that, I could have sunk into the ground, but it immediately reframed the way I saw the situation.

Years ago my wife and I were in Paris and I was operating on the premise that Parisians were very rude because they had seemed that way on my last visit. Naturally I had been rude back to them. My wife convinced me to try thinking of them as pleasant people and to act as if they were. To my amazement, most of the Parisians we met were delightful. What had changed? Only the way my brain was working.

You should now understand that reframing involves how you think about situations and then making a conscious choice about how you will react to them.

Let's start with your reaction to unemployment, a topic that is critical to most of us. If 10% of people are out of work you will probably tell yourself that unemployment is 10% and focus on the difficulties that creates. You don't have to think like this. You could mentally reframe it and decide that if 10% are unemployed, 90% of people must have jobs, in which case there must still be plenty of hope. What if youth unemployment reaches 40%? Then is it not still true that 60% (that's nearly two thirds) of our young people **do** have jobs?

We are not playing with words here. You have the choice of seeing it any way you choose. However, the benefit of changing your thinking like this is that you start to get your mind off the worry of unemployment. This enables you to start focusing on ways to make sure you end up in the 60% that have a job, not the 40% who don't. Look around you and listen quietly. You will notice that "most people" waste their time focusing on the problem and never try to find ways to solve it.

Do you remember what we discussed in chapter one? It's not what happens to you, but how you react to it that matters. You cannot change what is. What you can change is the way you respond to it. This will then change the way you act, which will in turn lead you to a more favourable outcome.

We have introduced the concept of reframing early in the book because its understanding is vital to your success. Here are some examples for you to think about to make sure you understand it properly:

(1) A young person breaks up with their boyfriend or girlfriend. The choice is to regard that as the end of the world and mope around for months, or to regard it as an occasion to find somebody else. It may even be an opportunity to take an overseas holiday or find a job somewhere else that may lead to all sorts of exciting possibilities.

(2) A family goes for a holiday to the beach and experiences a week of wet weather. One family might sit around and complain about the weather for a week, another family might see it as a chance to go to the movies, play games and spend time together.

In *The Law of Success* Napoleon Hill uses the re-framing concept without giving it a name. He states:

"You are fortunate if you have learned the differ-ence between temporary defeat and failure; more fortunate still, if you have learned the truth that the very seed of success is dormant in every defeat that you experience."

This means if you look hard enough you will find an opportunity in even the worst of happenings.

On his audio recording *How to be a No Limit Person,* psychologist Dr Wayne Dyer tells the story of the woman who was attacked, raped, shot through the head and left for dead in the boot of a car. By some miracle she survived this dreadful incident, but is now blind. She laughed as she told him that now she does not have to look at her children's untidy bedrooms. We know this is an extreme case and she is showing a strength of character that few of us could match. However, nothing can change what happened to her. She has had traumatic experiences that have left her blind for the rest of her life. Her only choices are to make the most of what she has left or to give up. She has chosen to take a positive view.

You will see reframing everywhere once you become aware of it. Thomas Edison, the inventor of the light bulb, spent years trying to find the secret. Once a reporter asked him how it felt to fail 10,000 times. His answer was "I haven't failed 10,000 times—I now know 10,000 ways not to do it."

A friend of Noel's received a summons for $50,000 for alleged negligence in his business. Instead of ranting and raving about having to fight the action in Court, he took it as a warning that there were defects in his systems that needed fixing. Maybe that summons saved him from a future summons for a much larger amount.

Here's another story.

Two men stopped at a newsstand to buy a news-paper. The man behind the counter was one of the rudest people they had ever met. One of the men continued to be pleasant to the paper seller, which prompted his friend to remark, "How can you be nice to such an awful person?" The answer was "You don't think I'm going to let a fool like that control my actions, do you?"

Notice how he kept control of the situation in his own hands and how that changed the way his friend looked at the incident.

James says...

Our family used to play a game when we faced a rude person. We would put all our efforts into making that person smile and after a little work we usually succeeded. I regard it as a great way to keep control of your emotions. Wayne Dyer tells about taking his family to a restaurant and being served by a rude waiter. Dyer said to the waiter, "I can see you are stressed out—we are in no hurry. Why don't you take a few minutes to get yourself together and then come back to serve us." You can imagine the effect on the waiter.

Playing "games" goes much further than having fun. By reframing the situation into a challenge and looking at it in a new way, you are transforming yourself into a person who can take control of any situation. No longer are you a robot reacting mindlessly to anybody who wants to press your button—you have changed to a person who is able to control your emotions and take charge.

As you meet successful people in all walks of life you will notice that most of them have the philosophy of "that was meant to be" when an unwanted incident happens. W. Clement Stone, the President of Combined Insurance Inc., greeted all bad news with the words "That's good", and then he would think about ways to find something good out of the bad that had happened.

When you reframe a situation you take control of it. By asking yourself "How can I turn this to my own good?" you are putting your creative powers to work towards finding a solution instead of wallowing around complaining like "most people" do. Suppose you apply for a job, or for a promotion, and miss out. Yes, you have missed out and, for today, you can't do a single thing to change that. However, you could analyse why you missed out and plan to do better next time. It is also possible that missing that opportunity allows you to take advantage of a better one that is waiting around the corner.

The ability to reframe a situation in a positive manner will be a critical factor in your search for success. In the next chapter we'll consider how your brain works and how you can start to think highly of yourself.

The vault:

- You can change your life by changing the way you look at it.
- Reframing involves analysing how you think about situations and then making a conscious choice about how you will react to them.
- By reframing the situation into a challenge and looking at it in a new way, you are transforming yourself into a person who can take control of any situation.

7

WHAT DO YOU THINK ABOUT YOU?

The greatest discovery of my generation is that human beings can alter their lives by altering their attitudes of mind.

William James

You now know the magic formula for success and understand that the approach you take to life has a huge role in deciding your future. However, knowledge is not enough. To succeed, you must believe that it is possible for you. In this chapter we'll think about the key factor that will make or break you—it's called "self-concept".

How do you genuinely see yourself? Ask a room full of teenagers, or even adults, and you'll probably hear a stack of self-derogatory comments. Words like "average" or "not much". Many will even take it a step further and use terms like "too skinny", "too dumb", "too tall", "too clumsy". There seems to be a feeling in our society that it's wrong to think good things about ourselves. There is also a custom that you show hidden admiration for your friends by saying something nasty about them—to their faces of course.

It's a pity so many people think like this because how we see ourselves affects almost every aspect of our life. This image of ourselves is called self-image or self-concept.

Remember, in the last chapter we discussed how to reframe a situation to see it better; now we will consider reframing the way we see ourselves. To do this we will examine how self-concept is formed, how it develops and how we can change it. If you can master this, and it's not difficult, your success is guaranteed.

Our self-concept begins to take shape as soon as we are born and, sadly, for most of us it is a downhill cycle. We are born with a brain that is more powerful than the world's largest computer but, like a computer, our brain has to be programmed. We are not born with instruction books tied around our waists so "most people" go through life accepting whatever programs society wants to give them. Because we live in a world that is basically negative, most of the programs are negative too. This trial and error method of programming the brain with whatever happens to come along takes its inevitable toll and as a result some people go through life oblivious to what they might have become if they had only followed some simple rules.

Think of your brain as a blank memory chip that is continually bombarded with messages from the day of your birth. These are stored till the day you die and your brain reacts to every situation in the light of what is stored in memory.

To help you understand self-concept, think about an imaginary person we'll call Ms X. She just happened to be born with a tall, strong body into a household where the family tended to be big eaters and ate a lot of junk food. Naturally she copied this pattern and developed the same eating habits as the rest of the family; her brain had been programmed since birth that this was a normal diet. Because of her naturally solid build and her bad eating habits she became quite plump.

Her mother, Mrs X, was also plump from the same combination of a naturally large frame and bad diet, but she always desired to have a figure like the slim models featured in all the magazines. She was forever going on crash diets to try to look like these so-called glamorous people but the diets only lasted a short while and she was back on the junk food path again. Ms X often heard her mother say, "I've got no willpower—I just can't stick at anything." Mr and Mrs

X often had violent arguments, particularly when he had been drinking too much, and Ms X would hear her father call her mother names like "fat", "ugly" and "stupid".

Ms X's brain was soon programmed with the beliefs that slim was better than plump, being overweight meant you were ugly as well as stupid, anybody from her family was doomed to be overweight, and furthermore they had no willpower. It got worse. Ms X's schoolmates teased her about being overweight and by the time she was 14 years old she regarded herself as a total loser—fat, ugly and stupid. That was her self-concept.

Contrast the case of Ms Y who was born with the same build in similar economic circumstances. Her parents knew the importance of good diet and taught her from an early age that she was lucky to have such a strong, healthy body and that she should take care of it with the right food. The parents praised her qualities and never made derogatory comments about each other in front of her. From the day she was born she was treated as a special person by her parents and taught that, although life had its ups and downs, she was smart enough to handle whatever life dished up to her.

Ms X and Ms Y were almost identical on the day they were born but by the time they turned 14, their belief in themselves was radically different. Why? Solely because of the way their brains had been programmed since birth. Their behaviour matched their individual self-concepts. Ms X saw each problem as further proof of her stupidity. Ms Y saw problems as a challenge and an opportunity to learn. Ms X reached a stage where she felt there was no point in trying because anything she did try was certain to fail. Failure was her program.

You will read more about self-concept in a later chapter about positive mental attitude but the above example should help you to know how self-concept develops. The input from the world around you programs your brain and you start to act in accordance with those programs. These actions are in line with that programming and therefore reinforce it.

We develop our self-concept mainly by what we tell ourselves, by what others say to us and from situations we observe and take part in. Napoleon Hill tells how he regarded himself at age nine as a criminal in the making because his father had always treated him like one. Luckily his father remarried a great woman who reversed all the damage his father had done. When Dad introduced the young Napoleon as "the meanest boy in Wise County", she replied, "You are wrong ... he is a very alert and intelligent boy and all he needs is some worthy objective toward which to direct his very good mind."[4]

---

4   Hill, Napoleon. Grow Rich with Peace of Mind. (1967:11) Fawcett Crest, New York.

That was the turning point in Napoleon Hill's life—when, at the age of nine, he received his first compliment.

To further illustrate the point, we will tell you something about Noel's life, because in his experience it is the illusions of life that play a major role in fouling up our self-concept. As the song goes:

> *I've looked at life from both sides now,*
> *From win and lose and still somehow,*
> *It's life's illusions I recall;*
> *I really don't know life at all.*[5]

Noel says...

As I've mentioned, my father was a pig farm manager so naturally I was the "pig farmer's son". For some strange reason I got the idea that pig farmers were a lesser form of life than other farmers and I always felt embarrassed about telling people what my father did. My brother and I were never short of love or food but there was very little spare money. I have a vivid memory of the family sitting down at a restaurant called the Green Dragon in Surfers Paradise in 1950 (I was 10) and having to leave without ordering because our parents decided we could not afford to eat there.

---

5   Mitchell, Joni. "Both Sides Now" (1967).

Because I went to a small country school, there weren't too many opportunities to play much sport and my spare time was spent helping around the farm, which I always enjoyed. When I got to high school I discovered that all those who had already been playing sport for their school went into the sports team and those of us who were left over were given a softball bat and left to amuse ourselves. This immediately produced two types of people in my mind: "sporting stars" who were in the school team with big badges on their blazer pockets and "the non-sporting types" who had no sporting ability.

By the age of 14 I had a self-concept of being the pig farmer's son who was too clumsy to play sport. It's an awful feeling to be the last one picked when the sides are being chosen.

I found my escape in books but the problem with the books I read is that they all starred the superhero that deep down I wanted to be. It's bad enough to feel you're a person with no sporting ability from a deprived background, but once you start comparing yourself with all the heroes in the novels you are in real trouble. I did not know then that comparing yourself with others is one of the silliest things you can do.

My parents were ardent Royalists and Mum kept a scrap book in which she carefully gummed items about the Royal Family that she clipped from the papers. There's nothing wrong with that, of course, but it meant my parents strongly believed in a class system where the classes didn't mix. Apparently we were on the middle rungs and, for my own sake, it was drummed into me that people from our end of the ladder shouldn't try to climb up it much further. If we did try, the unavoidable outcome of trying to rise above our station would be frustration and disappointment. Luckily they also programmed me that people from our station were "good honest workers". That bit of mind programming has stood me in good stead until this day.

We don't know where you're at right now and we don't know the background you come from. However, it is almost certain that you have suffered your fair share of negative programming. Your parents might have split up and you could still be feeling the effects of it; maybe you've suffered abuse or have been bullied or teased. Perhaps you trusted somebody who took advantage of you. Almost certainly you have suffered the insecurity of adolescence.

Actor Michael Caine described his teenage years like this: "My nose was too big. The thinner you got the bigger it looked ... these problems all sound insignificant to adults, but to teenagers they take on an almost suicidal importance. Teenage children spend a ridiculous amount of time looking in the mirror as their facial structure convulses, rises and sinks like a pot of boiling porridge."

"When all this is covered with a strategically placed veneer of pimples, you have the reason why most children never smile between the ages of 13 and 19. It is a terrible period for most kids."[6]

ADJUSTING YOUR SELF-CONCEPT

Self-concept does not develop overnight nor can you change it overnight. What you **can** do is start to make changes slowly and eventually the results will show. The following ideas will help you do it.

(1)　Be aware that self-concept does exist and that yours has been programmed since birth. This awareness will help you start to change it.

(2)　Don't become angry about the negative programming you have received so far and start blaming other people for doing it to you. You cannot change what has passed and you are

---

6　Caine, Michael. What's it all about. (1992:40–41) Random House.

wasting time by dwelling on it. Everybody who has affected you was, in turn, affected by somebody else and it is as unfair to blame them for their actions as it is for somebody to blame you for yours. You will spend the rest of your life in the future, which is where you should be concentrating your efforts.

(3)   Be thankful for some of that negative programming because it may be a source of motivation for you. Some psychologists have referred to your negative experiences as the "burr under the saddle" that spurs people on to success. Frank Sinatra said, "The best revenge is massive success", and you can act on that by reframing your negative experiences with the words "I'll show them". As a friend once said, "Opposition is a help not a hindrance. Kites rise against the wind, not with it."

(4)   Understand that your self-concept develops from what goes into your brain. Therefore, take great care to prevent any more negative programs taking hold. You probably haven't realised the main input to your brain is "self-talk" which is what you say to yourself continually. A good example is what people say when they are playing sport. You'll hear statements like "My backhand is no good" or "I'm off my serves today" or "My putts are letting me down".

If you want to prove to yourself how self-concept works, reinforce the other person's concept by saying, "Yes—it's a pity, isn't it?" and watch what happens. We guarantee they'll get even worse. You could then try to help them improve by praising their good shots. Depending on the sport you prefer, read one of the Timothy Gallwey Inner Game[7] books that show you how to excel through the use of mental techniques.

Gallwey states: "It was pointed out that the desire for improvement is natural, that man has a unique tendency to interfere with his own development, and that the primary form of interference is the forming of limiting images about himself and of trying to prove his own worth ... Why are we so eager to accept beliefs about who we are, to identify with our performance appearance and roles?"[8] Exploring these ideas through books will help you to become more conscious of the way your self-concept affects every action you take.

(5) Resolve that you will never again say anything negative about yourself. There is almost a tradition that we play down our achievements, but we have never heard any of the real winners we know knocking themselves. If somebody pays you a compliment, accept it with a simple "thank

---

[7] Galley, Timothy The Inner Game of Tennis, The Inner Game of Golf, The Inner Game of Skiing and The Inner Game of Music Pan.

[8] Gallwey, W.T. and Kriegel, Bob. (1977:106) Pan.

you" and don't feel the need to add something derogatory about yourself to show how humble you are.

Noel says...

I met up with a friend once who I had not seen for many years. When I asked what he was doing he replied, "I'm a Judge". "That's great," I said. I was shocked by his answer: "It's nothing. I'm just a District Court Judge."

(6) Start going out of your way to help self-concept of other people by giving them praise and encouragement and never knocking them. Nothing will improve your own self-concept like helping that of others.

Noel says...

Never underestimate the power of your words on other people. I had words said to me when I was a teenager that still hurt today even though they were said more in fun than malice. Conversely I owe much of my success to encouraging words. I vividly remember walking out of Mass one Sunday morning to hear the Parish Priest Kevin Aspinall say to me quietly, "I've been watching you. You will go a long way". I was 40 when that happened and the words came at a time when I was going through a time of great self-doubt and inner conflict. Few experiences have given me such a boost.

(7)   Establish a pattern of small successes and build on them. You will only harm your self-concept if, after reading this book, you set yourself huge impossible goals and then fail to achieve them. Our aim is to get you thinking like a person who can solve problems and overcome difficulties. Every small success you can notch up will give you the strength to go for a larger one.

(8)   Read as many autobiographies as you can. By doing this you will have the privilege of sharing the thoughts of achievers. You will discover they had exactly the same doubts, fears and bad programming as you have experienced. For example, in Michael Caine's autobiography he relates how he believed that only handsome dark-haired Americans could be film actors because he had only watched a certain type of American movie. This concept started to change when he discovered Spencer Tracy who was fair-haired and not good looking in the conventional sense. He continues "The clincher came when I saw my first European movie. It starred ... Jean Gabin and he featured everything that I thought could hold me back: fair hair, a big nose, and a small mouth. He was the biggest star in France, so everything was now possible." In fact, Michael Caine was the first major movie star to wear glasses in his films.

When you read statements like his you will appreciate how your own progress is being held back by illusions.

James says...

Some years ago I was fortunate enough to meet a well known business consultant, author and public speaker named Sergio Carlo Maresca over a coffee. We spoke about what we'd done recently and what each other had planned for the future in regards to both career and personal development. I was immediately impressed by his forward and honest insights on life.

I was at somewhat of a crossroads and he enquired as to what I was interested in pursuing for the future. I mentioned a strong desire to get into public speaking, but at that point lacked the direction to do so.

He said I'd be a fantastic speaker and promised to recommend me for a speaking engagement almost a year away. I agreed, half expecting to never hear anything again. Ten months later, I was contacted regarding an event and ended up speaking in front of 700 people. Although terrified backstage beforehand, it remains one of the most rewarding experiences of my life—and it never would've have happened if it wasn't for his inspiration and encouragement.

There are many books and courses available to help reprogram your brain. The message of this chapter is that it is highly likely that you have a low self-esteem because of the bad programming your brain has received up to this point. When you have finished this book you will be well on the way to installing good new programs, which will replace the old ones that may be holding you back now. At this stage it's enough that you be aware of the extraordinary influence of self-concept.

The vault:

- We develop our self-concept mainly by what we tell ourselves, by what others say to us and from situations we observe and take part in.
- You cannot change what has passed and you are wasting time by dwelling on it.
- Never again say anything negative about yourself.
- Nothing will improve your own self-concept like helping that of others.
- Every small success you can notch up will give you the strength to go for a larger one.
- Read as many autobiographies as you can so you can share the thoughts of achievers.

8

WHAT YOU GIVE IS WHAT YOU GET or THE LAW OF SOWING AND REAPING

There are 10 weaknesses against which most of us must guard ourselves. One of these is the habit of trying to reap before we have sown and the other nine are all wrapped up in the one practice of creating alibis to cover every mistake made.

Napoleon Hill

The message of this chapter is simple—we can only get out of life what we put into it.

Don't we human beings have strange thinking habits? We would never sit in front of an empty fire-place hoping, by some miracle, that heat would come out it. We know if we wanted heat we would find some dry wood, build the fire and then strike a match. Yet we are often guilty of hoping for many things in life to happen before we take the necessary steps to bring about the desired outcome. It's called trying to reap the harvest before we have sown the seeds.

Haven't you wanted top grades without doing the work, sporting honours without doing the practice, a fit body without doing the exercise? Of course you have—that's human nature. No wonder the exercise machines on late-night infomercials that promise an amazing body and six-pack abs for five minutes work are so popular. Ray Kroc, the founder of McDonald's, tells the story of a famous musician who was accosted by one of those chatty society women at a cocktail party. "I'd give anything to play like you," she said. "No, you wouldn't" was the reply, "You wouldn't be prepared to practise for hours, to give up the social life, to exist on a pittance while you were trying to make your mark—that is what made the difference."

The good news for you is that "most people" spend all their life wishing for things they haven't earned and only a few, that's right about 10%, make the effort to get them. Every Saturday night millions of people will be sitting round their television sets waiting for their "numbers" to come up. Sure somebody usually gets lucky and scores the big prize but many of those million dollar winners are broke again within a few years. In any event, can you afford to let your future depend on a million to one chance? The odds of your number coming up are definitely not in your favour.

There are two rules you need to know about sowing and reaping. The obvious one is:

(1)   You cannot reap before you have sown.

The less obvious one is:

(2)   You always reap far more than you sow.

Nature is clever. She knows it would be a waste of your time to plant a cup of corn if all you got back at harvest time was another cup of corn. No, plant a cup of corn and you may well get back bags and bags of corn. Better still, if you ate some of the corn and planted the rest, those bags of corn seed you plant have the potential to produce thousands upon thousands of bags of corn.

In *Making Money Made Simple,* in the chapter titled "The Torch", Noel tells the story of a poor boy Orison Marden who found out about the secrets of success in 1870 by reading *Self Help* by Samuel Smiles.[9] Marden became the founder of *Success* magazine and Napoleon Hill was one of his first reporters. Hill then wrote *Think and Grow Rich* which has been read by millions of people and inspired the likes of W. Clement Stone, Jim Rohn and Og Mandino. Literally millions of

---

[9]   Samuel Smiles's book Self Help was first published in 1857. It was translated into 17 languages and has been one of the bestselling success books of all time.

people have been helped to a better life because the writings of Samuel Smiles sowed one tiny seed in the brain of Orison Marden.

Unfortunately the law of sowing and reaping works in both the positive and the negative. If you sow a few weed seeds, you end up with a huge crop of weeds. Therefore the more "good" seeds you sow, the more "good" results you harvest and the more "bad" seeds you sow, the more "bad" results you have to cope with. What happens if you don't sow anything? It will be more weeds, not corn, that will pop up.

Examples of this are the people who drop out of high school because the work is tough, and then try to find jobs to bring in some money, and then make no effort to improve their skills. They attract a paltry harvest. As a result of never gaining worthwhile skills, they spend their whole lives in lowly paid jobs or living on welfare. Thus, they cheat themselves out of millions of dollars of extra money they could have earned if they had made the effort to improve their knowledge.

You must also be vigilant in protecting what you sow. There will be many things that try to impede your road to wealth—"most people" would rather have you on their level so they can feel better about themselves. But ask yourself "What seeds am I planting if I give into these external forces?" Just as a farmer uses scarecrows, pesticides and immense care when tending the harvest, you must apply the same dedication and foresight to avoid the negative pull of those around you. Your rewards will be far greater for doing so.

Many years ago when Noel worked in the bank a teller "borrowed" a few dollars from the cash drawer. He was found out and the bank administration ordered his instant dismissal. It was only a small amount of money, and he had intended to put it back next day, but it cost him a promising career.

What excites us about sowing and reaping is the way small seeds can grow and the way a seed planted now can produce a crop many years later, often when you least expect it. This is why it is important to keep sowing "good" seeds all the time, for you never know when they will suddenly burst forth into a crop.

Noel says...

One day, when I'm rich, I want to be a GREAT philanthropist.

...And you've already started as a modest one, yeah?

I made a speech several years ago to a group of car dealers and their staff. A new car salesman named Roy approached me and handed me his business card with the words, "When you want to buy a new car give me a ring". I took one look at the card and noticed that he worked for a dealership that was 50 kilometres away. When I told him I always bought locally he smiled and said, "When you have experienced my service you will buy from me". Some feeling inside me made me keep the card and six months later I was shopping for a car. I tried the local dealership but was put off by a rude salesman who told me an obvious lie by trying to pass off last year's model as a current one. That's one of the traps of buying a car in January—that difference

of one month means a big difference when you come to sell it.

Shortly after, I phoned Roy. He sold me a car and has been looking after my cars since. Servicing is not a problem because he always has my car collected from home and provides a loan car for the day. I have referred many other people to him and I am sure they, in turn, have referred others. The act of handing me a business card (and, in doing so, sowing a single tiny seed) has given Roy a harvest of over 100 sales.

We could fill this book with stories like the ones above but we are sure you have got the message. Now you should ask yourself what good and bad seeds you are sowing and remember that many bad seeds take a long time to surface.

Many older people now have problems with scores of tiny skin cancers that keep popping up on their faces and arms because they spent too much time in the sun without protection when they were young;

thousands of people die every year as a result of slowly destroying their lungs with cigarette smoke. Most people reach retirement age without enough money to live on because they never "got around" to starting an investment program until it was too late.

You are young and have the opportunity to start planting seeds now that will provide a harvest beyond your expectations. In the next chapter we'll teach you how to do it.

The vault:

- We can only get out of life what we put into it.
- Ask yourself what good and bad seeds you are sowing.
- Be vigilant in protecting what you sow.
- It's never too early to plant seeds that will change your life.

9

GOALS—WHAT YOU SET IS WHAT YOU GET

What an immense power of life is the power of possessing distinct aims. The voice, the dress, the look, the very motions of a person define and alter, when he or she begins to live for a reason.

Elizabeth Strut Phelps

The message in this chapter is that the most extraordinary things start to happen when you set goals.

Noel says...

I was sitting in a plane waiting for take-off when the flight attendant whispered to me, "I wish I was in your shoes—look who is going to sit next to you". I looked up and there was the handsome form of ironman Grant Kenny. Grant turned out to be a quiet person, as many high-profile people are when you get to know them, but, as I had been studying success for nearly 20 years, I couldn't miss the chance to ask him what his secret was. He thought for a second and said, "Setting goals, I guess".

A week later I bumped into Kevin Carton who was then the Australian head of the Sheraton Hotel chain. Kevin is not just a successful executive, he was also an Olympic hockey champion. I asked him the secret of his success. Guess what the answer was? "Setting goals, plus the ability to keep a smile on my face when the game got tough—that really used to bug the opponents."

We have spent thousands of hours reading books and listening to audio recordings about success and have found there is one factor on which they all agree. That, is the importance of setting goals—the ability to decide what you want and then make a detailed plan to go after it. If you can master the art of doing that your success is guaranteed, for you have literally given yourself the power to design your own future.

When you set a goal you make a statement about something you wish to happen. However, a properly set goal is much stronger than a wish, it's a commitment. Contrast this to the everyday chatter of most people: "I wish I was happy", "I wish I could stop work", " I wish I could travel". These are not goals; they are dreams that will probably never happen. There is nothing wrong with dreaming, but far too many resign themselves to the dream when, with a little effort, they could have had the real thing.

The moment you commit to a goal, strange forces come into play and incredible things start to happen around you. It seems that once you set a goal your brain works on it day and night, even when you are sleeping, working out ways to bring it about and attracting events and people to you that will help make it happen.

You can set goals in many areas of your life. Your goal may be to buy a car, have a holiday in Europe, lose six kilos in weight, buy a house, pay off a debt, win the local tennis championship, get a promotion at work or complete a study course.

It works like this every time: you desire an outcome, to reach it takes some effort on your part, and you will have to give up something to get it. If you are saving for a car, house or holiday, it involves taking money from each pay packet and putting it aside. You have to give up the fun of spending now so you can achieve your goal. It's been called the ice cream/bicycle syndrome. You forgo eating the ice cream today so you can have a bicycle tomorrow.

Similarly you must devote time to exercise and healthy eating to lose weight, and put in many hours of practice or study if you wish to win the tennis match or complete the study course. There is always something to give up. Notice how it all gets back to the law of sowing and reaping. Those who do not want to pay the price of giving up in order to get, finish with nothing.

SETTING GOALS

We'll now take you through the steps of setting a goal. We'll use the example of having a goal to buy a car.

(1)   First you must clearly define exactly what you want. The brain cannot act on a vague goal such as "I want to travel".

You must have a clear picture in your mind of what the car will look like. This includes make, model, colour, number of doors, features, etc. Find that car's brochure either from a car dealership or through an internet search, and make sure it has at least one coloured photograph of the car. Then stick it up on your bedroom wall where it will be the first and last thing you see each day. If you are choosing a second-hand car you should be able to print a description and photos from one of the many car websites.

Take a camera along to the local car dealership and have one of the staff take a photo of you sitting in the car of your dreams. Make sure it is the same model and colour as the one you want.

(2)   Name the date on which it is to happen. It is no good saying, "I want to buy a car". That's another wish. You must say something like "By 20 January 201X I will own a white Toyota Model XXX."

(3)   Draw up a plan to get it. Suppose the desired date is 24 months away, the cost of the car is $9,000 and you have $4,200 saved up now. The difference is $4,800 and you have 24 months to find it. Therefore you need to save $200 a month. Can you do that? To find out, you'll have to draw up a budget (covered in a later chapter).

What happens if you do all the figures but the plan does not seem possible in the time frame you have set? For example, you list your income and all your expenses and decide there is no way you can save the $200 a month you need. Now you have reached the interesting part—you must stretch your mind to try to find ways to achieve the goal. Ask yourself if the goal is realistic, even though it's a bit of a challenge. If it is realistic you will have to think of ways to find the extra money. If that's not practical you will have to modify your goals.

Let's imagine it is realistic but you just don't have that $200 a month available. It's then a matter of cutting your spending or earning more money. Go over your budget and see what you can prune out of it. Are you buying lunches when you could be taking them from home? Could you get a lift to work instead of using public transport? Can you cut down on clothes? Are you wasting money on cigarettes?

Now think about ways to increase your income. Is a second job possible? Can you get a job at the car dealership washing cars and have the payment taken off the car price? Do the neighbours need somebody to mow their lawn or to babysit their children?

The best part about learning how to set goals is the change that takes place in you as a human being. Once you think about achieving your goals you start to focus on ways to solve problems. This is in stark contrast to "most people" who spend their life talking about the problems and never get around to finding any solutions. By concentrating on the solutions instead of the problems you distance yourself from the herd.

You have now started to become a human being who has the ability to set goals, to make plans to achieve them and to adjust those plans if circumstances change. In other words you are starting to take control of your life. Congratulations, you are well on the road to success.

WHY GOAL SETTING WORKS

Goal setting works for two reasons.

(1)   Setting goals gives your mind a focus. Think about what happens when your goal is to save for a car, you need $400 a month to do it and the photo of the car is on your wall as well as in your wallet. Sure, you may be tempted to break out and waste some money but you will clearly understand that by having the "ice cream" now you will delay "riding the bicycle". You will also find the goal of owning the "bicycle" will become so dominant that the wish for the "ice cream" will be far easier to fight.

Noel says...

When my wife and I bought our home we set a goal to pay it off in three years. To help us stay motivated we kept a statement of the loan account pinned to the pantry door where it caught our eye every time we took something out to eat. That always kept us on track and the joy of watching that big loan come down gave us far more pleasure than spending the money on clothes or going out.

On a trip to Tasmania we found ourselves browsing through a craft shop where we noticed a beautiful Huon Pine salad bowl with an inlaid pewter top. It was a magnificent work of art and we were both keen to buy it despite the price tag of over $500.

We stood for over half an hour admiring the amazing craftsmanship. However, our dominant goal then was to pay off a large loan we had on one of our investment properties so we could free up the money we were paying in interest to use for more holidays overseas. We finally decided to forgo the pleasure of buying the bowl because it was not in line with the goal of reducing the debt. The goal had enabled us to avoid the temptation. The price of the bowl was tiny compared to the debt we were paying off, but we knew that once you start giving in to small temptations the goal loses its importance. You then fall into the trap of "Well, just this once" and it starts to happen over and over.

If you have neglected an assignment and abruptly found the deadline approaching, you would have experienced the power that comes from goal setting. Suddenly working on that project takes over your thoughts and you find a power and concentration you never experienced until the deadline drew near. You become focused on the task to the exclusion of all other thoughts. This is what goal setting is all about.

COMPETING GOALS?

The problem with setting goals is that you can become trapped among competing interests. You may want to buy a car, have a holiday, buy a house, a new outfit, party with your friends, enrol in a study course and win the sporting event. What do you do?

Noel says...

The solution is to try to put together a list of goals that will work together. For example, when I was studying accounting after I was married, I studied from 7pm to 11pm from Monday through to Thursday. This gave me Friday night and the weekend for other activities. Each study night I went for a 30-minute jog at 9pm and followed it with a quick shower. This accounted for the exercise goal but it also gave me a bonus. The run and shower halfway through my study freshened me up for the rest of the night.

I also got a dose of motivation because I always jogged along the same route. Every night I would pass a house and notice the owner sitting in the same chair watching television. I told myself, "In four years I'll have my degree and he'll still be sitting in the same spot wasting his life."

James says...

  When I was 19 years old I was saving for an overseas holiday, but was spending too much money out with my friends on weekends. My savings were being eaten away by my social life. I then began working in a nightclub on most Friday and Saturday nights doing bartending. After a few weeks I was amazed at how much my savings had grown. Rather than spending $100 out with my friends, I was actually earning the $100 and was able to put it straight into the holiday savings.

  So, maybe it's time to think outside the box a little:

– *Combine a sporting goal with an exercise/healthy eating goal (or even a financial one). For example, focus on increasing your running ability through better eating and increased training. You may also find that eating healthily will make you more focused on your running because you're reminded of your sporting goal every time you eat. Winning the high school cross country championship will be a breeze when you're reminded of your goal five times a day! Your diet will also improve because you'll need the right food to fuel your body.*

– *Combine a savings goal with a study goal. For example, you could opt to stay home and complete a minimum of three hours study five nights a week. Although you'll likely miss out on social events from time to time, you'll be forgoing the "ice*

cream" for the greater reward of the "bicycle". De-
vote your time to bettering yourself and improving
your education and you'll save money on restau-
rants, drinks and other entertainment costs.

Remember to keep a balance in your life, so don't neglect going out and having fun with your friends; just do it sensibly and in ways that align with your goals. As you can see from the above examples, managing your time more efficiently can help more than you ever imagined.

START WITH SMALL GOALS

This book is all about helping you to make minor changes in your life that will lead to bigger changes later. Because you improve your self-concept through a series of little successes, it is best to start your goal-setting program with small goals that have a strong chance of achievement. Once you have mastered these you can move onto bigger ones.

For example, if you have several small debts you may set a goal to pay one of them off quickly, say, in three months. Perhaps there is a piece of sports equipment you want, like a pair of running shoes. Set yourself the goal of saving up for it. Just practise the techniques we showed you of writing it down, stating a time for realisation of the goal, and focusing your mind on it.

While you are doing this, remember that goal setting is useless unless you take the right actions to achieve them.

There is no point in setting a goal to buy a car in 18 months if you continue to spend all your money on shopping and entertainment; you are fooling yourself if your goal is to lose weight yet you still snack on pastries and chocolate. Ask yourself "Does my behaviour match my goals?" If the answer is "no", you had better do some quiet thinking about where you really want to go in life.

Don't be frightened to use tricks to help you stay on track. For example:

- Exercise with a friend. This will make you turn up at the right time, you can motivate each other to do better, and you may even compete against each other to see who gets the best results.
- Leave your credit cards at home. This will stop the impulse buy and keep you focused on your needs rather than your wants.
- Only do your grocery shopping *after* a meal. This will keep you from buying junk food and other un-necessary items.

When writing a book we usually arrange the publication date first to provide us with a firm deadline to write to. Otherwise we fall into to the "We'll start next week" trap, shuffle papers for months and never get around to doing anything of substance.

THE SALAMI TECHNIQUE

A variation of starting with small goals is to use the "salami technique" which gets its name because it is like slicing thin strips off a piece of sausage. You simply figure out what your goal is and then break it down into a series of smaller sub goals. Then each sub goal becomes a series of more realistic and achievable goals that, when achieved, equates to the original larger goal.

We use this technique when we're writing a book because a book, like accumulating a million dollars, is far too big a goal to grasp. It is much easier to first make a list of the chapter headings and then work on the sub goals of writing each chapter.

James says...

Courses on "how to write" often encourage you to come up with the topic sentence of each paragraph, then several supporting points, then a concluding sentence—there's your paragraph. Writing a number of topic sentences and paragraphs sounds much less daunting than a 2,000-word essay.

In *Making Money Made Simple* Noel gives the example of the 10-step ladder to a million dollars. The ladder is only 10 steps and the first step is to save a mere $2,000. "Most people" take one look at the million dollars at the top of the ladder, decide it's all too difficult and go back to watching television. The smart ones know you can only climb a ladder one step at a time and focus on the $2,000. When they have climbed that rung they move to the next goal, which is to accumulate $4,000. That is also easy because it's only a matter of putting together another $2,000, which they now know they can do.

It is in our nature to be encouraged when we complete a task and to be discouraged when we fail to complete a task. By working on many small sub goals that combine into a large goal we manage to keep up our enthusiasm as well as finally accomplishing great things.

You now know what goal setting is and why it works. Some of the books listed at the back will give you more information. We'll now move onto three essential skills that will speed you on your journey to success.

The vault:
- The common thread in all success stories is the importance of setting goals.
- Live your goal by putting tangible reminders in the areas where you spend the most time.
- Make your goal as specific as possible.
- By concentrating on the solutions instead of the problems you distance yourself from the herd.
- Start with small goals. Making minor changes now will lead to bigger changes later.
- Use tricks to keep you on track, like exercising with a friend.
- Adopt the salami technique—break a big goal down into a series of smaller ones.

10

THE THREE ESSENTIAL SKILLS

Do a little more than average and from that point on your progress multiplies itself out of all proportion to the efforts put in.

Paul J. Meyer.

As you know, you will get out of life whatever you put into it—good and bad. This chapter focuses on three skills that will help you into a leadership role, for it is through leadership that you can increase your opportunities.

Our aim is to help you become a person who is in charge of your life and who can make things happen instead of being at the mercy of other people's whims. As Jim Rohn said, "Either you are making plans or somebody is making plans for you."[10] Therefore you should cultivate those habits that will transform you into a leader instead of a follower. Leaders are paid more, have more opportunities for self-development and there are more openings available to them.

---

10 Rohn, Jim. From his Challenge to Succeed Seminar.

There are three special attributes that will help you become a leader. None of them are particularly difficult, they don't need any special aptitudes and they are available to almost everybody. The big plus is that you can pick up these skills quickly and, when you master them, they will probably make a great difference to your life in a short time.

The three attributes in leadership development are:

1. Get into the habit of going the extra mile.
2. Acquire some basic sales skills.
3. Learn to speak well in public.

As you can see, there is nothing too hard about any of them. The first is a habit that you should be able to pick up in a month, and the other two are skills that are easily learned. Just don't underestimate the way they can change your life and, as you read this chapter, remember that "most people" never attain them. Consequently, anybody who makes the effort to master them automatically goes to the head of the field.

GOING THE EXTRA MILE

Noel says...

Some years ago, my wife and I were driving home from the annual speech night of my old school—Salisbury State High School, and we were pondering over the way fate had worked in that time. It had been 38 years since my first speech

night at the school and I had returned to present the prizes and make a speech. I doubt if anybody in 1954 would have dreamed that 38 years later I would have been on the stage giving out the prizes but, against all expectations, it had happened. We tried to focus on what I had done right, as opposed to the hundreds of things I had done wrong, in those 38 years and discovered two factors that I am sure helped me along the way. They were going the extra mile and being a non-stop learner.

As Ray Kroc, the founder of McDonald's, said, "Are you green and growing or ripe and rotting?"

My parents had instilled in me how important it was to always give of my best and it had always seemed sensible to me to keep learning and discovering new things. However, it wasn't until I read Think and Grow Rich *that I discovered that going the extra mile has always been the hallmark of successful people.*

You see it everywhere if you look for it. Take this example when I was at my golf club to practise on the driving range. The young assistant pro smiled as he threw half a dozen extra balls into the bucket and said, "Better make sure it's full to the top". On the way home I crossed the toll bridge and, because it's my custom to go the extra mile, I gave the toll keeper a cheery smile and a greeting. Naturally she responded in a similar fashion. "Don't forget you've only got one trip left" she said as she inserted the card in the slot. That's the way going the extra mile works. You put it out and you get it back. The beauty of it is that it requires no special skill; all you have to do is form the habit.

Consider the following incident. It is not earth shattering, yet it has stuck in my mind since the day it happened and I have recounted it to audiences around the world.

The time was 7.50am on a Tuesday, and I was staying at the Sheraton Hotel in Townsville. I was heading down to breakfast and was keen to pick up a copy of the Cairns Post *newspaper because I knew it would contain a photo and an article about a speech I made there the day before. I said to the bellboy, "Where is the paper shop? I am after a copy of the* Cairns Post. *" He told me the papers were sold from the small store in the lobby but it did not open till 8am. "No* problem," I replied, "I'll pick one up after break-fast."

I went to breakfast and promptly forgot all about it until 8.05am when the bell boy appeared at my table with a newspaper. "Here's your Cairns Post, " he said and disappeared. Now that's what I call going the extra mile.

Later I reported the incident to Elin Power who was the training manager of the Sheraton at the time and she told me the staff had been trained to try to second-guess what the guests wanted and to surprise them in just the way the bell boy had surprised me. Was that a big deal or not? It was only a small action and anybody could have done it. Yes it was a big deal, it is memorable and it causes a ripple whenever I mention it to an audience. That is because it was so unusual!

Contrast this to the case of a 16-year-old girl who came to our office to do some temporary work. She was after a permanent job and, unbeknown to her, we were looking for a permanent junior. She was a good worker and would have been offered the job except for one bad habit. Every afternoon at 4.55pm she was packed up and waiting to leave. That is the opposite of going the extra mile. She was never offered the job.

A friend of mine is an executive of a large company. He says, "When we are hiring staff we look for the person who has done a lot of extracurricular activities while they were at school. We *don't want somebody who thinks life is a 9 to 5 job."*

By going the extra mile you ensure you get noticed, which means you will usually be first in line for any special jobs that come along. These extra jobs give you the chance to learn more skills, to show more of your abilities to others and to move faster and faster along the road to wealth.

ACQUIRING SALES SKILLS

Unfortunately, far too many people have an image of "selling" as something cheap and nasty and regard salespeople as inferior beings who are not to be trusted. That's an unfortunate belief. Sure, there are some shonky hardsell merchants about but most salespeople are honest and fill a vital role in our community. In most situations their role is to identify a problem, find the solution and convince the customers the solution is suitable for them.

Imagine you were considering an overseas holiday. You would expect the sales consultant in the travel bureau to find out where you wished to go, work that in with what you wanted to spend and then plan an itinerary that would suit you and give you pleasure. If you are looking for a new outfit, the salesperson's job is to find something that you will feel good in, and in your price range.

In short, selling is the art of taking charge, knowing what to do and convincing others to take action. It requires similar skills to leadership. Top salespeople are among the highest paid people in the world because they are rare—few will put in the effort that is necessary to provide a high level of customer satisfaction.

There's another reason too. The pay of most salespeople is often directly related to their performance. That's right—they are paid according to the sales they make. Most people would find that too uncomfortable, but if you're serious about improving yourself, doesn't it make sense to be paid what you are worth? That way you can earn more than others if you are good enough.

If you think about it, nearly all highly paid jobs have an element of selling in them:

- A doctor selling a patient on the idea of giving up smoking.
- A coach convincing the team they can win.
- A professor selling the need for more funds for the department.
- A manager selling the employees on different work practices.
- A public relations expert selling the media on the idea of using a story.
- An author convincing a publisher to accept a book.
- A parent selling the child on the idea of extra study.

They all involve persuading another person towards a course of action that should be of benefit to that person.

Please don't confuse this with the idea of "hard sell" where indifferent or unscrupulous salespeople try to convince people to buy something that may be wrong for them just to make a sale. Yes, it does happen, but you will discover those people never seem to get far in life because they are ignoring some basic principles that will be revealed as you read further.

Your local library will have many books on basic selling, and your parents, employer or friends may have access to some of the good audio programs that are available. A simple internet search will allow you to see or hear some of the great salespeople of our time. See what you can find.

Developing sales skills will show you how to gain the trust of others, ask probing questions to get to the heart of a problem, handle troublemakers and persuade others to a course of action. These are all leadership skills that will point you to the top.

LEARNING TO SPEAK WELL IN PUBLIC

Do you know that most people would rather contract a serious disease than get on their feet and speak to an audience? Winston Churchill said, "The three most difficult things for a man to do are to climb a wall leaning away from you, to kiss a girl leaning away from you and to make an after-dinner speech."[11] As a child, Churchill was painfully shy and stuttered but, through preparation, mastery of technique and practice, he became one of the greatest orators of the 20th century.

It's hard to understand this fear of public speaking because most children love to perform in public. Apparently at some point in our lives we become self-conscious and start being concerned about making a fool of ourselves.

You will find hundreds of books about public speaking in your library but to do it well you need experience, a sound knowledge of your subject and communication skills. These are not hard to acquire. Knowledge of your subject will come automatically as you continue studying your chosen field and you can gain experience while you are learning the communication skills.

---

[11]   Churchill, Winston. Reported in "Idea Bank" a supplement to The Executive Speaker Newsletter, October 1992.

The easiest way to start is to join a Toastmasters Club or Rostrum Club and become an active participant. Speak to established business leaders in your community, or someone you look up to, and ask for their recommendations. When you attend one of these clubs or gatherings, you will meet other frightened and no longer frightened people who are all learning to speak in front of a group.

Of course, you are likely to be terrified at first. The following slogans might help you overcome that fear:
- No pain, no gain. (Jane Fonda)
- Feel the fear and do it anyway. (Susan Jeffers)
- Whether you think you can or think you can't, you're right. (Henry Ford)
- Nothing in life is to be feared, it is only to be understood. (Marie Curie)
- You can't discover new oceans unless you have the courage to leave the shore. (Anonymous)
- Thinking will not overcome your fear, but action will. (W. Clement Stone)

You'll often find that standing up in front of people and starting your presentation is the hardest part. It's not very often that a person gets a few minutes into their speech and then gets nervous. Work on memorising the first 30 seconds of your speech and you're assured of a great start, which will get rid of any remaining fear in your body.

It's well worth the effort. As each speech passes you will feel more at ease. The time will then come when you look forward to standing up and holding forth. Then you will be able to help others overcome their fears as you develop your skills even further.

Once again, think outside the box. Does your job require interaction with customers? If so, your employer might be more than willing to fund some (or all) of the costs of a public speaking course, which will significantly improve your self-development.

Regard this moment as one of the many crossroads in your life—the road you take will have a vital bearing on where you finish. You can choose to think "I could never stand up and speak in public" and give in to your fears. This will make you even more scared to try anything new and may well deprive you of the chance to discover much of the potential you never knew you had. On the other hand, you may think, "I'll give it a go; I've got nothing to lose and everything to gain." Do this and you have just taken a big step on the road to success.

Think about it. We know that achievers do what "most people" are not prepared to do. If you make the effort to join a public speaking or debating group, you have faced a fear and overcome it. Furthermore, you have done something that most people are not prepared to do and have thus moved further down the path of self-development.

Remember—not trying guarantees failure; trying gives you a chance of success.

The vault:

- Through leadership you can increase your opportunities.
- Key steps in leader development are: getting into the habit of going the extra mile, acquiring some basic sales skills, and learning to speak well in public.
- Going the extra mile is the hallmark of successful people.
- Do something that most people are not prepared to do.
- Not trying guarantees failure; trying gives you a chance of success.

11

FINDING YOUR INNER POWER

Everyone has inside them a piece of good news. The good news is that you don't know how great you can be! How much you can love! What you can accomplish! And what your potential is!

Anne Frank

The message in this chapter is that you have many skills that you have not yet developed. If you develop your skills, you will expand the value of the service you can offer, which will increase your rewards in life.

Noel says...

In 1978 my life changed when I went to a breakfast to hear a talk by an American named Jim Rohn who I have mentioned several times in this book. I didn't want to go to the breakfast because at that stage in my life I foolishly thought I knew everything (after all I was 38 years of age) but something inside me drove me there. The theme of his lecture was "Don't wish it were easier—wish you were better". It really hit me.

If you are like "most people", and like I was at the time, you have probably spent a lot of time wishing life was easier. You have almost certainly wished you did not have to cope with such ongoing problems as study, finding and keeping a job, money, and handling complex relationships with loved ones. That's a natural feeling. Unfortunately, you will find the problems don't vanish as you grow older—you just get a different set of problems. Hopefully by that time you'll have learned some of life's lessons and will be able to handle them a little better.

Listen to the conversations of those around you and notice that much of it is in the category of "I wish life was easier". It is full of complaining about problems and wishing that they would go away but, as no time is given to finding solutions, the situation seldom improves.

However, you now know about reframing and once you reframe your attitude from "wishing life was easier" to "wishing I was better" you can start to work on the skills that will make it better. When you do this you move the focus from worrying about problems to trying to find solutions. You can then start to take charge of your life instead of being a helpless victim in the control of others.

The solution to almost every problem is to educate yourself to handle it better. This process is called "self-development" and means that you make the time and effort to learn new skills. This will help you in several ways:

(1)   New skills open up a new world of opportunities for you. These include job promotions, a chance to travel and the possibility of starting your own business.

Noel says...

When I read Think and Grow Rich *I set a goal to be involved in my own business within 100 days. I was 34 and by this stage in my life I had experience in banking, conveyancing, personnel work, accounting, tax, property development and marketing. These all combined to make me a useful participant in a building business and within 130 days I was in partnership with a builder. He brought his building skills and experience to the venture and, combined, we were a highly effective team. The time I had spent in self-development paid off.*

(2)   New skills boost your self-esteem. Because you feel better about yourself, you perform better. This makes you feel even better about yourself and you perform even better—so the cycle continues.

James says...

This is one of the most powerful things I have ever learned.

When you feel better about yourself, you share that joy and happiness with the world. If someone's having a rough day, a quick smile or a polite gesture on your behalf might be enough to turn it all around for them.

Develop the skill of being happy, and your inner power and positive energy will radiate to those around you. Once you practise this enough so that it happens automatically, you'll notice people are happy and confident around you. And they will certainly enjoy your company because you have built your image as someone fun to be around.

(3) Your improved skills enable you to render a better service. As your rewards in life will always match your service, it must follow that by improving your skills you improve your rewards in life.

Noel says...

As a result of the years I spent working on improving my writing skills, I now earn extra money by writing articles in several newspapers and magazines. Learning to type has enabled me to write faster, and mastering the computer has given me extra time to write because much

of my writing is done on aeroplanes using a laptop. It doesn't bother me now if a plane is late and I find myself sitting around an airport. I just reframe it to "Aren't I lucky? I have got an extra half hour in peace that I can use to write some columns. That will give me more free time when I get home to spend with my family."

(4)　Opportunity favours the prepared. In every place of employment, from the factory to the opera, there will come a time when a key person becomes ill or unavailable, and then there is a frantic hunt for a replacement. If you are on the spot and have the skills, you are likely to get the chance to show your talents. Do the job well and you put yourself in line for promotion, which is another opportunity for you to learn even more skills.

(5)　In this modern and fast-changing technological world you will fall behind your competitors if you fail to keep up to date. Continual self-development is one of the best ways to pro-vide security because it ensures you are not being left behind.

A MAJOR ENEMY

Think about this one quickly: "How much does a TV set cost to own?" You may guess a couple of hundred dollars a year, but we believe the figure is closer to $1,000 a month. That is the money you lose while you are wasting time watching it.

Television is one of your greatest enemies be-cause it provides little by way of self-development for you, yet is a continual temptation because it is easy to turn on and even easier to leave on. The average adult watches over 1,000 hours of television every year—the equivalent of almost thirty 35-hour working weeks. Just imagine where you would be if you spent 1,000 hours a year in self-develop-ment?

Television is fine for a little relaxation but the problem is that many programs show an unreal world and serve to reinforce illusions about life. Al-so, the format of most programs is designed to appeal to the viewers with the lowest intelligence. The result is that your brain receives little or no stimulation.

In contrast, good books require some effort on your part and allow you to stop to think about the subject matter. They also allow you to re-read a passage if you wish.

James says...

We have found reading autobiographies to be a wonderful source of motivation, as well as one of the best ways to improve your mind, because they usually tell of the struggles and the feelings of inadequacy the authors went through. When we read this our own troubles fall into perspective and we can be inspired in the knowledge that other people have faced and overcome worse problems than we have had to endure.

After reading Lance Armstrong's It's Not About The Bike[12] *(where he describes his much publicised battle to overcome testicular cancer that had spread to his brain and lungs), it seems futile to complain about the traffic or weather. After beating cancer, Armstrong fought his way to full health and went on to win the Tour de France—widely regarded as one of the toughest and most gruelling sporting events in the world—a record seven times in a row.*

You should also think about effective learning, where you absorb material in the most efficient manner depending on what type of person you are. If you are a visual learner, try documentaries and educational magazines. If you crave a bit of peace and quiet, head to the nearest bookstore and see what you can find. If you are one of those

---

[12] Armstrong, Lance. It's Not About the Bike (2001) Barnes & Noble.

people who find "there just aren't enough hours in the day", download and transfer audio books and podcasts to your mp3 player so you can listen to them whenever you have a few minutes free.

Books have the power to change lives. The book *Self Help* by Samuel Smiles provided the motivation for Orison Marden to rise above his poor background, put himself through university and then start the publishing company that employed Napoleon Hill.[13] Clement Stone credits *Think and Grow Rich* with saving him from bankruptcy and inspiring him to become a billionaire. In *More Money with Noel Whittaker* Noel tells the story of the business executive who saved his job, his health and his marriage after reading *Success Through a Positive Attitude* by Clement Stone and Napoleon Hill. This same book gave the famous author Og Mandino the courage to face life when he was about to commit suicide.

BE DIFFERENT—MOST WON'T DO IT

Unfortunately, "most people" just aren't interested in self-development so if you take the time to improve your skills you will be in the minority. For example, in 1979 a survey looked at why 99.5% of the 3,500 workers in a truck assembly plant were not using a

---

[13] The full story is told in Making Money Made Simple in the chapter titled The Torch.

special education plan their union had won for them as part of a new work contract.[14]

In this plan the company was prepared to pay for any job-related training—"training that can even include college degrees." Less than 20 people out of 3,500 bothered to take up the offer. Why so few? We have little additional information about the experiment, but let's imagine what might have happened using our knowledge of human behaviour. The workers were probably in the low wage bracket because they had a low skill level and saw themselves as being trapped in that position because they were unable to pay for further education. Most likely they blamed

---

14 Brickwell, H.M. A study of the tuition refund plan of Mack Trucks, Inc. Hagerstown MD as reported in Adult Development and Aging by Rybash, Roodin and Santrock. (1979) W.M.C. Brown publishers.

their low income on their lack of education in the first place, which was the fault of their parents who had not been able to afford to send them to college. They were sure their lives would change if they did have education and convinced their union officials to fight for it.

Once they won free training they had a dilemma. Lack of money for self-development was no longer an excuse and they came face to face with the harsh reality that training meant study, doing assignments, attending lectures and giving up such luxuries as "after work drinks" and a night in front of the TV. They now faced the real reason for being in a low-paid unskilled job—their own lack of motivation.

Until then, most of the workers had probably used "I can't afford it" as the excuse for not trying to improve their skills. Once that excuse was taken away it is almost certain they found other reasons not to try.

Stop reading for a moment and write down how much you spend now on such items as clothes, music (CDs and mp3s), cigarettes, coffee, movies, haircuts, junk food, etc. Contrast it to what you are presently spending on improving your mind. If there is a huge imbalance, it might pay to consider that, in the long run, the money spent on self-development is what provides the money for the others.

Self-development takes time and effort but, as we said in the chapter on sowing and reaping, the rewards always far outweigh the effort. Only by working on your skills can you bring out the potential that is bursting inside you.

The vault:
- Move the focus from worrying about problems to finding solutions.
- The solution to almost every problem is to educate yourself to handle it better.
- When you feel better about yourself, you perform better.
- Improving your skills will improve your rewards in life.
- Opportunity favours the prepared.
- Think about the opportunity cost of watching television in contrast to spending the time on self-development.
- Only by working on your skills can you bring out the potential that is bursting inside you.

12

FAILING—THE ESSENTIAL INGREDIENT

The freedom to fail is vital if you're going to succeed. Most successful people fail time and time again, and it is a measure of their strength that failure merely propels them into some new attempt at success.

Michael Korda

The message in this chapter may scare you a bit, but it could also change your life. If you want to be successful you must expect to fail because failure is an essential ingredient in success.

Your reaction may be bewilderment. Right now you may be thinking the authors have lured me into reading almost half this book, have promised me success, and now tell me to expect continual failures. That is true, but the failures are ones that are going to help you to grow and develop your skills.

Let's think again about what we are trying to achieve. We are trying to make you stand apart from the herd and find the courage to gain the success that is your right. To do this you have to take actions to improve your knowledge and skills—in other words to move out of your comfort zone. This means trying a whole host of new things that you will probably find scary at first. These may include managing other people, handling difficult customers, taking up a sport, making a speech in public, undertaking a study course, or starting a business.

Noel says...

I vividly remember the time of departure when I made my first lecture tour on the cruise ship Oriana. It was June 1985 and I stood alone at dusk on the rear deck looking out as the great white ship left Circular Quay and slowly reversed until its stern was almost under Sydney Harbour Bridge. Then it blew its whistle and slowly edged towards Sydney Heads accompanied by several tug boats. The decks were crowded and everybody but me seemed to be with somebody else.

I did not know a soul and there are few occasions in my life when I have felt so scared

and so lonely. The usual silly negative thoughts ran through my head. "What if nobody wants to come to my finance lectures?" "What if those who do come don't like the lectures?" None of these fears came true and the trip was a great success. The point I am making is that even though I was 45 and an experienced speaker and traveller I was still plagued with worries. I am telling you about it here so you won't feel bad if you experience doubts and fears before trying a new experience. It's a natural feeling, but it almost always goes away once you start getting involved in what has to be done. Doubts are natural and so are failures—and I'll share some of those from my own experience too.

The only way to become competent in the area you choose is to learn about it and try to do it. Now, unless you are an exceptional person, you are not going to get it right first time. Even if you did get it right first time by some stroke of luck or genius, you would learn little by it—a real learning experience comes when it all goes wrong. It will be just like when you started to learn to walk, you tried many times, you fell over many times, but you never gave up. You kept on going and finally you made it. Sure, it was tough, but if you had not kept going you would be lying in that cot today thinking "I would love to be able to walk but if I try I might fall over and that might hurt. It's easier to stay here where it is safe and comfortable."

FINDING THE GOOD IN THE BAD

In all his books Napoleon Hill has stressed that every failure contains the seeds of a greater success. In her bestselling book *Pathfinders* Gail Sheehy points out that successful people are not those who have been insulated from failure, they are people who have faced and overcome failure. She notes, "Repeated to a striking degree in the histories of the most satisfied adults was a history of a troubled period during childhood or adolescence when many rated themselves as very unhappy. Some hit close to rock bottom ... Although an unhappy childhood is not something to be wished on anyone, those who struggle through it evidently do develop important personality skills."[15]

The possibility of a good outcome arising from a failure may be harder for young people to grasp than it is for us older ones because life is a bit like a novel—it takes time for the reader to see how the plot develops. Those of us who have been around for a few years have had the time to watch events unfolding.

Noel says...

Let me give you three events in my own life to explain what I mean.

When I was 29 I worked for a law firm. One day there was an argument at work and I resigned

---

15   Sheehy, Gail. Pathfinders (1981:60–61) Bantam.

in a state of temper. It was November and I was shocked to find that this is a time of the year when few companies hire new staff; they usually do it in January and February so they don't have to pay people over the Christmas break. After weeks of job hunting and a few weeks of tempo-rary work in a factory doing process work, I finally made the shortlist for a job that I was very keen to get—it was for a credit manager at a building company.

A week later when the "we regret your appli-cation was unsuccessful" letter arrived, I leaned against the refrigerator and cried my eyes out for about an hour. I was devastated then but now, when I look back on my life, I can see that if I had got the job I would not be where I am now. Another job came my way a few weeks later that led to far more exciting opportunities.

In 1979 I went through a divorce and suffered all the pain and self-doubt that divorce usually entails. I had a few female friends to go out with but there was nobody who looked like being a contender for the love of my life. On 1 April 1979 I had arranged to go to a function with one of them but she rang to say she had "a better offer" and our date was off. Naturally, I wasn't happy about being stood up but used the occasion to go on my own to a National Heart Foundation lun-cheon where I met a young lady named Geraldine who was (and is) the love of my life. We are now

happily married and have three beautiful children, Mark, James and Elizabeth. Also you'll find, as you persevere through relationships, that parting ways with someone, for whatever reason, is a great opportunity to reassess your goals. Like I said before, you might have your own example of how a great tragedy turned out to be one of the best things that's ever happened to you.

In 1986 I got involved in a property development venture that turned terribly sour. By the time we had worked our way through the problems I had lost almost half of the material assets I had spent 46 years accumulating. In money terms, the price was huge but what I learned in that venture has enabled me to make more than I lost. I must confess it was a frightening experience but I used the technique of reframing to help me cope. I told myself it would have been *much worse if one of my family had become critically ill or had been killed. Looking back I can honestly say I got more out of it than the price I paid for the "lesson".*

Certainly it can be hard to handle unhappy experiences and projects that turn bad on us, but it is the most effective way we can learn. Just as a piece of iron is made hard by being plunged red hot into a tub of cold water, so a person is made tough by facing and overcoming setbacks and problems. You will never reach your potential if you try to dodge life's challenges by avoiding new experiences.

GETTING THE MOST OUT OF YOUR MISTAKES

You will find that life continually sets you exams to find out what you have learned. If you fail an exam you are doomed to repeat the lesson until you know it. To get the most out of your setbacks, try the following:

(1) Analyse the situation and try to find out what went wrong. When you are doing this be strictly honest with yourself and don't fall into the habit of blaming others for the mishap. If you have been fired from your last three jobs or you are unable to have a compatible relationship with another person, it is likely the problem lies within you. Once you can face that, instead of trying to camouflage the reality by

blaming others, you are well on the way to finding permanent solutions.

(2) Practise the technique of reframing and tell yourself that what happened was obviously meant to be. Ask yourself if the incident has shown you a new direction. For example, if a job application is rejected think about whether you may be better suited to something else.

(3) Set out to find something good about the situation. For example, if you are booked for speeding treat the incident as a warning that your driving habits need attention and be thankful you were not involved in a serious accident.

(4) Treat it as an opportunity to reassess your goals. Does this mean some of your goals are unrealistic or is the problem simply a minor detour on your path to success? For example, if you fail to gain admission to the tertiary institution of your choice you may have to consider alternative routes to get where you want to go.

(5) Be aware that failure is only a temporary condition and there are many roads leading to where you want to go. Never forget the following statement by United States President Calvin Coolidge:

Nothing in the world can take the place of persistence.

Talent will not; nothing is more common than unsuccessful men with talent.

Genius will not; unrewarded genius is almost a proverb.

Education will not; the world is full of educated derelicts.

Persistence and determination alone are omnipotent.

The words "press on" have always solved the problems of the human race.

Noel has had it hanging in his office since he discovered it in 1976 and it has often given him comfort when the going got rough.

While you must accept failure, if you are to succeed it is also true that you need to set up a series of successes to boost your self-esteem and put you on a success path. Therefore, while it is important that you try new things, it is also vital that you don't put too great a burden on yourself by setting almost impossible tasks. If you keep at it, you will soon learn the difference.

The vault:
- Failure is an essential ingredient in success because it helps you to grow and develop your skills.
- You will never reach your potential if you try to dodge life's challenges by avoiding new experiences.
- Failure is only a temporary condition and there are many roads leading to where you want to go.

13

POSITIVE MENTAL ATTITUDE

Life is a self-fulfilling prophecy; you won't necessarily get what you want in life, but in the long run you usually get what you expect.

Denis Waitley

People with a positive mental attitude expect the best for themselves and other people in all situations. In this chapter you will learn about the importance of keeping a positive mental attitude and why it has such a big effect on the way your future turns out.

The problem with the term "Positive Mental Attitude" (PMA) is that many cynical people see it as sheer foolishness. They get a mental picture of a couple dancing for joy as they watch their house burning down with their family trapped inside it. This attitude towards PMA may be reinforced if you attend some of the sales meetings we have addressed and see people mouthing all kinds of optimistic slogans which, deep down, they don't believe. They leave making positive noises but never get around to doing what needs to be done to make their lives successful.

Norman Vincent Peale, author of *The Amazing Results of Positive Thinking,* explained it: "Positive thinkers do not refuse to recognise the negative; they refuse to dwell on it. Positive thinking is a form of thought which habitually looks for the best results from the worst conditions. It is possible to look for something to build on; it is possible to expect the best for yourself even though things look bad. And the remarkable fact is that when you seek good, you are very likely to find it."[16]

There is a well-known story about the two sales-people who went to a remote part of Africa in search of new markets. One reported there were no prospects of developing business because nobody wore shoes. The other cabled, "We have a massive untapped market—nobody wears shoes."

In simple terms, if you have a positive mental attitude you are an optimist who looks on the bright side of life and who expects most of the situations you face in life to have a favourable outcome. But! What if the initial outcome is unexpected, as it often is. Having PMA means you have faith that somehow the final outcome will still be a good one.

Notice how it is closely tied in to the material in the last few chapters. You can now reframe an unexpected result to put a good face on it, you know that failure is a vital ingredient in your success, and you

---

[16] Peale, Norman Vincent. The Amazing Results of Positive Thinking Reissued (1991:9) Cedar.

understand that every failure carries the seed of a greater success if you can find it. Once you combine that knowledge with the power of positive thinking, you can take action to produce the effect you want or to adjust your goals to go for a different outcome that will still be favourable to you.

We believe that having a positive mental attitude is a natural state because we have never seen a baby that didn't have a positive outlook on life. However, we seem to lose it as we get older because we become conditioned by the generally negative world around us. Because "most people" don't make it, they create a world where they will be comfortable. This is why newspapers and radio and TV stations prefer bad news to good news and feature the small number of bad things that happen. There is generally a headline on bad economic news or a disaster overseas, details of a car or plane crash, or a story about a murder.

You have probably noticed how the media tends to reframe all news to the negative, which is why the headline will be "Unemployment hits 10%" and not "90% of people still have jobs".

On one of his audio recordings US Senator Ed Foreman tells this story:

A young architect had just won a big contract. He went to a restaurant to have lunch to celebrate but as he sat down saw a newspaper on the next table. The huge headlines were "Depression predicted". He got such a shock that he cancelled his meal. When the proprietor asked the reason for the sudden change of heart he replied, "Look at the headlines—there is a depression coming. I had better save my money."

The restaurant owner was so surprised that he rang his wife immediately and said, "There's a depression coming. Cancel that new dress you have ordered." The wife promptly telephoned the dress shop owner and told her that she had to cancel the order because there was a depression on the way. Naturally, this worried the dress shop owner and, after a quick discussion with her husband, she decided to cancel the building contract for the planned extensions to the dress shop. She rang the builder to pass on the bad news who immediately decided to cancel all the jobs he had planned for the next year. His first call was to the young architect who had started all this off, to tell him his services were no longer required because "a depression is coming".

Bitterly disappointed, the young man slunk back to the restaurant to drown his sorrows. This time he was in no hurry and picked up the paper that was still lying there. To his amazement he discovered it was an old paper dated 20 years ago and had been left there by a previous customer who had found it when he was cleaning out some old boxes. The "depression" had all been in the young man's mind, but its effects were still as real as if the paper had been printed to-day.

This story displays the power of negative thinking and should alert you to the importance of keeping a positive attitude. How do you become a positive person? The best way is to make it a habit but like all other habits it needs to be practised until it is firmly in place.

James says...

Our feelings in life seem to come and go in waves. One day you'll have several waves of happiness but the next day you might get hit with a wave brimming with negativity and unhappiness. And these waves certainly aren't limited to days. Sometimes your good wave could last a week, a month or a year, but inevitably a few bad waves will roll through every now and then—that's life. Be ready for the bad waves, understand them, and your PMA will get you back on track in no time. Convince your friends to focus on the good waves and the results will become evident very quickly.

Negative thinkers fear the worst and, therefore, subconsciously probably don't try as hard. It usually takes time and effort to produce a worthwhile result and there are often setbacks along the way. How could you possibly stick with a project if you believed you would fail?

There is more to PMA than the value of ongoing motivation that it provides. You should also be aware of the principle of positive and negative attraction, as espoused by Napoleon Hill. His theory is that electrical waves in the brain attract to you what you fear or truly desire. Because negative thinkers put out negative vibrations, they find that the outcomes they fear come true exactly as they predicted. Consequently, their belief that they are always "cursed" by bad luck is reinforced. They are on a downhill path.

Jim Rohn believes that "success isn't something you pursue; it's something you attract".

In *Pathfinders* Gail Sheehy writes, "A person with a positive outlook is more likely to attract friendship and love which promise in turn the richer intimacy and emotional supports that characterise overall life satisfaction ... people who allow themselves to become soured on life often set in motion a self-reinforcing cycle. Their anger or self-pity becomes so off-putting that it deprives them of the friends and help they otherwise would deserve."[17]

Now think about those who have read what is in this book and are starting to put it into practice. They have set practical goals, they are discovering how to make them happen and they are working hard to develop their skills, which is building their self-esteem. They don't worry about following the crowd because they understand that "most people" are going in the wrong direction. They are not concerned about making mistakes because they know that failure is at worst an opportunity to learn and can therefore face the future with confidence.

Watch how it all works together. Their brains are putting out the right "vibes", they are being noticed because of the extra effort they are putting in, and life is steadily improving for them. As their lives start to get better they create a success pattern for themselves on which they can build. Their positive mental attitudes have helped them to do all this and, in turn, the results of their positive thinking encourage them to maintain a positive attitude.

As Albert Einstein once said, "Weakness of attitude becomes weakness of character."

---

[17] Sheehy, Gail. Pathfinders (1981:21) Bantam.

The vault:

- If you have a positive mental attitude you are an optimist who looks on the bright side of life.
- Make a habit of becoming a positive person.
- When faced with a difficult situation, look on the bright side and attract positive experiences into your life.
- The results of your positive thinking will encourage you to maintain a positive attitude.

14

GIVE IT A TRY

Eighty percent of success is showing up.

Woody Allen

The message in this chapter is that you should try to have as many learning experiences as possible. You may have heard the saying "luck is what happens when preparedness meets opportunity". Therefore, it should follow that the better and wider the preparation, the more chance there is for opportunity to pop up, with "luck" to follow.

Have you ever gone to the beach on a summer's day when the weather is slightly cool despite the season? The ocean looks wonderful and you walk across the sand and try the water with your toe. Feels icy. You go through the same old pattern of "Let's go in", "No, it's too cold", "Well, maybe". Then the sheer joy of the day overcomes you and you take the plunge. The first reaction might be a scream as the water hits your back, but in less than 30 seconds you are bobbing along happily saying, "It's not too bad, after all".

Most of life's situations are like that. You face a barrier and are initially put off by the apparent difficulty of it. However, you finally find the courage to cross it and then almost always discover it wasn't nearly as hard as you thought it was going to be. These barriers are important points in your life and you will keep striking them as long as you continue to grow. They are important because your reaction when you meet each one affects the way you face other barriers.

If you stop and refuse to take the plunge you are reinforcing behaviour that will probably happen again at the next barrier. You will find it harder and harder to make progress. On the other hand, if you do act, the next barrier will be easier to attack because you are forming habits that will help you make progress. As the great doctor and writer Maxwell Maltz said, "Close scrutiny will show that most ... 'crisis situations' are ... opportunities to either advance or stay where we are."

In 1991 the grazier Sara Henderson was named Australian Businesswoman of the Year. Her autobiography is an inspiring read and gives a graphic account of the hardships she faced throughout her life. These include a severe car smash when she was 16, almost dying while giving birth to a child, being trapped in a raging typhoon near Hong Kong, and facing bankruptcy when her husband died, leaving her with a huge string of debts. She writes, "The knowledge you gain from your experiences, good or bad, would not have been gained if you had not had the experiences! You must experience to grow, with growth comes knowledge and with knowledge you change."[18]

Noel says...

I now spend much of my time appearing on radio programs and making speeches to large audiences. Let me assure you I wasn't born with a talent for that; in fact I once had a speech impediment that made my early years a misery. My speaking career started at age 21 when my employer, the Bank, offered to pay for any staff who wished to improve their public speaking skills by joining Rostrum—a public speaking club. As far as I know, I was the only person who took up the offer. Everybody else was too scared of speaking in public. Naturally, I was as frightened as the rest of them but I was prepared to make the effort to learn this valuable skill.

Going to Rostrum was a terrifying experience at first, and I had a particular problem in that my knees used to shake violently whenever I got up to speak. It was hard going at first but as I persevered it got easier, and after a few months of embarrassment even my knees stopped knocking.

---

[18] Henderson, Sara. From Strength to Strength (1990:304) Macmillan.

Time passed and through hard work and study I found myself working in the Bank's International Division dealing with foreign currencies. The Bank asked for a volunteer to give a monthly lecture on foreign currency at the staff training school. As usual, I was the only volunteer but I saw it as a further chance to develop my speaking skills and to "pose" as a VIP once a month by being driven to the school in a large, black, chauffeur-driven car.

Later, when I was running a building and real estate company, the Real Estate Institute offered six people (including me) the chance to go to Canberra for a two-day weekend course on public speaking run by the renowned speaker Doug Malouf. Three refused, but the rest of us saw it as a further chance for skill development. The course was even better than we had hoped and we all benefited greatly from it.

Learning is an exciting process because the moment you acquire a new skill, or a piece of *knowledge, a chance comes up to put it into use.*

Just three days after I returned from the course the ABC rang to ask if I would do a talk-back radio session for three Tuesday nights between 10pm and midnight. Naturally, I agreed and, using the knowledge I had gained at the Doug Malouf course, managed to convince the local Sunday paper to do a feature story promoting the program. I had pulled the double—the ABC and the paper were both promoting the segment. Thus, the program received maximum publicity and the phone lines ran hot.

While all this was going on I also made the time to sharpen up my writing skills by putting a weekly 400-word column in the local paper. This forced me to find a topical subject each week, write about it in an interesting way and to meet deadlines. All very useful skills.

A few weeks later another local station 4BC rang me to see if I would like to host a real estate and finance program between 6am and 7am on Saturdays. Once again I accepted the offer but figured that nobody would have the slightest interest in finance at that hour. I was wrong. Many people who are interested in finance are early risers and many others forget to turn their clock radios off on Friday nights. In any event I developed a loyal bunch of listeners as I further honed up on my talkback radio skills. Even more impor-

tant, I was being kept in touch with what the public needed to know.

Eventually I started writing a weekly finance column in Brisbane's The Courier Mail. *One fateful morning a woman rang the radio program to tell me she liked what I was saying and asked me to name some books in which she could read more about the topics I spoke about and wrote about. I promised her I would check out the bookstores during the week and tell her and all the other listeners next Saturday morning.*

What do you think I discovered? There was nothing in the book shops that covered finance in a simple way. Sure, there were American books showing you how to turn $1 into a million quickly and easily (!!!) and thick academic books with tiny print and loads of meaningless graphs that looked too boring to open. However, there was nothing that covered the vital subject of finance in a way that enabled the average reader to benefit from it. I decided to write Making Money Made Simple, *the book which became an international best-seller and changed the lives of many who read it.*

This may have been a long story but sometimes, when I am about to give a speech to a huge audience, or get ready for a radio or television program, I wonder where I would be today if I had not accepted the Bank's offer and volun-

teered to join that public speaking club many years ago.

Most people will never get out of their comfort level and try something new, yet it is only by trying new experiences that we can reach our full potential. It doesn't matter if the experience is helping behind a shop counter, changing a tyre, selling raffle tickets, trying 10 pin bowling or experimenting in the kitchen. Somewhere, someday, it will be useful to you even if it shows you what you **don't** want to do. My wife and I loved to run the Devonshire Tea stall at the school fete when our children were in primary school because just one day a year of standing on our feet working so hard gets rid of any urges we might have to own a restaurant.

Anne Lewin was a young woman when she and I met about 20 years ago. She had a small shop called "Lady Leather" in Fortitude Valley in Brisbane where she made leather hats and belts. The shop grew and she expanded her range by making other leather goods. She changed course and started selling real estate but soon found that was not to her liking and started designing and making elegant lingerie. She has done so well that the Anne Lewin name is now known worldwide and Anne lives in New York running the fashion empire she has created. It all happened because Anne has never been afraid to "give it a try".

We'll bet when you were a child you weren't frightened to give it a try. If you were like all the children we know, you were into everything—eating dirt, running naked on the beach in winter, poking your fingers into the dog's mouth, talking to strangers.

Now you're probably different. Now you know about fear and embarrassment and rejection and peer pressure and that daredevil-try-anything attitude has been replaced by a feeling of "What will happen if I try this and it hurts, or it doesn't work, or I end up feeling silly?"

If you feel like that, as most people do, it might be a good time to reflect on the words of William Shakespeare: "Our doubts are traitors, and make us lose the good we oft might win by fearing to attempt." When you face a new situation ask yourself, "What is the worst thing that can happen if this goes wrong?" Very often nothing more than a bit of temporary embarrassment.

The vault:

- Try to have as many learning experiences as possible.
- It is only by trying new experiences that we can reach our full potential.
- In hindsight, most things were a lot easier than they seemed at the start.

15

UNIVERSAL LAWS

The gifts that one receives for giving are so immeasurable that it is almost an injustice to accept them.

Rod McKuen

This chapter will explain two fundamental laws that are understood and followed by truly successful people. They remind me of the concept of love—difficult to define and measure but still very much in existence. You may question what follows, or it may confirm what you believe, but in any event it will pay to know about these laws. You may pay a heavy price if you break them.

THE LAW OF GIVING AND RECEIVING

James says...

Let's first talk about the law of giving and receiving. It has been put in many forms. My father always told me, "If you do a good turn you'll get two good turns back." My primary school teacher taught us the Golden Rule: "Do unto others as you would have them do unto you." The Chinese philosopher Lao-Tzu said, "He who obtains has little. He who scatters has much." I hear many people say now, "What goes around comes around." The meaning remains the same no matter how you say it.

Both of us, and and most of our friends, believe in what we call the great "bank in the sky". You do good turns whenever you have the opportunity and think of them as placing deposits of good turns in some mythical bank. Then when the time comes, as it always does, that you need a good turn or a helping hand, you will find that somebody will be waiting to help you. Usually the good turns don't come from the same people you have helped, but they certainly come back. Sure, we know it sounds weird, but it works for our friends and for our family.

As your awareness grows and you read more books on success, you will notice the concept cropping up continually. In his audio recording *Transformation—You'll See It When You Believe It* psychologist Dr Wayne Dyer tells about the mechanic who came to his beach house to fix the refrigerator. The mechanic was loaded down with problems, which he talked about at great length. After an hour had passed Dr Dyer had given him a complete counselling session as well as numerous books and audio recordings free. The mechanic was amazed that anybody could be so generous and exclaimed, "Mister, how come you can give so much away without going broke?" Dyer smiled as he replied, "When you know the answer, you won't have to ask the question." You see he knew about the law of giving and receiving—the more you give away, the more you get back.

In *Law of Success* Napoleon Hill points out that the Golden Rule is based on the principle of sowing and reaping, which ensures that you will reap more than you sow, both positive and negative. If this is so obvious, why do so many people fail to practise it? Probably because there are two types of people—those who focus on scarcity and those who focus on abundance.

The ones who focus on scarcity see the world as a dangerous jungle. They work on the principle that everything is in short supply and only those who jump in quickly and knock everybody aside will survive. They spend their lives in constant fear—fear they won't have enough to live on, fear somebody else will beat them to a promotion, fear they will get sick. You can recognise them because their lives are in such conflict that they seldom achieve any sort of happiness.

Noel says...

I met a person with a severe case of scarcity thinking when I was giving a speech in Fiji. Contrary to popular perception, it's often lonely when you are far from home in some other country and I had been trying to find a golf partner to fill in an afternoon. A widow from Chicago decided to join me and we set off for the golf course that was nearly 30 kilometres from the hotel. She spent the entire journey to the course worrying if there would be a timeslot to play available for us. When we got there she was worried that it might rain. During the round she worried all the time that she would lose her ball. And, as we neared the final hole, she expressed concern that we might not find a taxi to take us home.

On the way home she worried we might be late for dinner and during dinner she did not have a glass of wine in case she got too drunk to pack. She will never re-marry lest the new husband dies like the first one did, and she won't go out with men in case she gets hurt in a relationship. When I left her, she was concerned that all her clothes would not fit in her suitcase!

The opposites are people who focus on abundance. They have acquired a positive mental attitude that helps them to reframe a bad situation, they understand that failure is no more than a learning experience and they believe that somehow things will work out for the best. Because they feel this way, they are usually optimistic happy people who are always ready to share with others.

As you delve further into this subject you will find that most students of human success believe we attract into our lives what we focus on the most. Those who focus on abundance attract prosperity; those who focus on scarcity attract all the bad things. Do you notice how this goes round and round? Because the prosperity thinkers have an optimistic view of the world, they automatically practise the law of giving and so are assured of receiving.

One of the most famous essays in success literature is *Compensation* by the American poet Ralph Waldo Emerson. Napoleon Hill calls it "a must for people who want to understand themselves, understand the world and find wonderful peace of mind that will stay with them".[19]

Emerson writes, "Men suffer all their life long under the foolish superstition that they can be cheated. But it is as impossible for a man to be cheated by anyone but himself, as for a thing to be and not to be at the same time."[20]

[19] Hill, Napoleon. Grow Rich with Peace of Mind. (1967) 36th printing (1991:139) Fawcett Crest, New York.

[20] Emerson, Ralph Waldo. Emerson's Essays (1951:86) Thomas Y. Crowell Company New York.

You can call it what you will: the Golden Rule, the Law of Sowing and Reaping or the Law of Compensation. By any name, it means that we finally get back more than we put in. That's what Emerson meant when he said we can only cheat ourselves. By being too lazy or too indifferent to sow, we forfeit the great harvest we could have reaped.

THE LAW OF OPPOSITES

We call this one the law of opposites. That simply means you often have to do the opposite of what seems logical to get the result you want. Here are some examples:

- The more a farmer takes from the land, the less it returns in the long term. The way to get the most out is to put the most into it.
- In golf you make the ball rise by hitting down on it. You make it go faster by slowing down your hand action.

- The way to be lovable is to be loving. A person who is frantically trying to make somebody else love them is a sorry sight. It's like the child belting the kitten to make it purr.
- The harder we try to think, the less chance we have of coming up with the right answer. It will come when our minds are relaxed. You must have gone through the experience of having something you were trying to remember on the tip of your tongue and trying harder and harder to remember it without success.

Kahlil Gibran wrote, "I have learned silence from the talkative, toleration from the intolerant, and kindness from the unkind."[21] Emerson said, "The only reward of virtue is virtue; the only way to have a friend is to be one." [22]

At Bert Weir's Centre Within course[23] Noel learned the best way to handle feeling unhappy was to find somebody to help, and the best way to boost self-esteem was to try to make somebody else feel

---

[21] Reported in Bits & Pieces (The Economics Press, Fairfield New Jersey) September 17, 1992 at page 12.

[22] Emerson, Ralph Waldo. Essays 1841. Friendship.

[23] Until his death in 2009, Bert Weir conducted courses at the Relaxation Centre, Brisbane. You can find much of his material in his book You Were Born Special, Beautiful and Wonderful: What Happened? published by the author.

good about themselves. That is probably why the happiest people we know are those who spend time helping others.

In the section about successful negotiation in *More Money with Noel Whittaker* Noel points out the secret of finding the best outcome is to look for a "win/win" situation where both parties get what they want. Let's look at a practical example of this in the light of what we now know about the law of opposites.

You want to borrow the family car to visit your friends, but Dad wants it to take to golf. If you both focus only on what you want, the outcome is doomed to failure. A bitter argument is almost certain to occur with Dad driving off to golf in a most unhappy state, leaving you without wheels. You will probably be miserable for the rest of the day and Dad will most likely play a dreadful round of golf and come home in a worse mood than when he left. You may then regard him as a cruel thoughtless parent and he may regard you as a problem child.

Imagine what would happen if your thoughts were focused on making sure Dad got to golf safely and in a happy frame of mind, and his thoughts were focused on ensuring you had a great day out with your friends. After a friendly talk, during which you both worked out ways to help the other gain what they wanted, you might agree that you could drop Dad at the golf course on the way to your friends' place and one of his golfing partners could give him a lift home. Everybody is happy, the outcome is satisfactory for both and the relationship is strengthened. Obviously this has huge benefits for both of you and it all happens because you choose to focus "out" and not "in".

The two laws in this chapter are a part of all religious beliefs and have been known to the human race for centuries. They are as valid now as they have always been and you will notice them occurring everywhere as your awareness develops. Your happiness will grow as you start to work with them.

The vault:

- The law of giving and receiving—the more you give away, the more you get back.
- You will reap more than you sow, both positive and negative.
- We attract into our lives what we focus on the most.
- By being too lazy or too indifferent to sow, we forfeit the great harvest we could have reaped.

16

IT'S UP TO YOU

You need only choose ... then keep choosing as many times as necessary. That is all you need to do. And it is certainly something you can do. Then as you continue to choose, everything is yours.

Vernon Howard

This chapter could also be called "Facing Reality". Its message is that your life is very much in your hands.

That's a harsh way to start, but you must understand it if you are going to make something of your life. Read the quote at the top of this chapter again and think about it. You are where you are now because of the choices you have made to date—the smart choices and the thoughtless choices that all of us make. We are all human and have all done many positive and negative things. However, that is in the past. Where you will be in the future depends on the choices you make from now on.

When children are learning to ride a bike they usually suffer many hours of wobbling about, falling over and getting up again. Finally something clicks, it all comes together, and they have no trouble riding a bike again. Learning to take charge of your life is like that. If you continue along the path of self-development, a moment will come when you understand that you are in charge of your life. Once it clicks you will never be the same again.

Wouldn't life be scary if you weren't in control—if life was a lottery, and you had no influence over the outcome? It would be like speeding along a busy road in a car with no brakes. Fortunately, it's not like that. You do have brakes, but the road of life has hundreds of intersections and each time you come to one you have to pick which turn to make. If you keep choosing the wrong turn you end up on bad roads. Once you find yourself in the area where all the bad roads are, the situation worsens. Finally, the only choice you have is between a bad road and a worse road.

To illustrate that point, let's think about somebody we'll call Tommy who went to an overcrowded school. He could choose between paying attention in class and doing his homework, or ignoring both the teacher and the homework. He chose the lazy way and his work got behind that of his class mates. When his problems were discovered he had a choice of going to extra classes to catch up, but he chose to watch TV instead. He finally dropped out of school.

He then had the option of taking a training program, but chose to stay home. He could not get a job, got in with a bad crowd and was enticed to "borrow" a car for a joyride. He ended up in Court. He was let out on probation, but chose to break it. Eventually he was sent to jail where the only choices left to him were serving out his time or trying to escape.

Mary got her first job at 19 and had a choice of saving some money and spending what was left, or spending all of her pay and buying clothes on credit cards. Because she had chosen to borrow on her credit card to buy clothes she then faced the choice of buying no more until the debt was paid off, or increasing her borrowings. She chose to increase the debt, after all the repayments on $2,000 are only $25 a week, and continued spending as if there were no tomorrow. She was $4,000 in debt after 18 months. Her friends had been saving up to go on an overseas holiday and asked Mary to go with them. Because she had no savings, she chose to borrow another $5,000 on a personal loan.

When she returned from overseas, she got a nasty shock when she discovered how much debt she had accumulated. Her friends urged her to seek financial counselling but she chose not to. Finally, the strain became so much that she was unable to focus on her work and she lost her job.

Do you notice that both Tommy and Mary had plenty of chances to take the best road? However, each time they decided on a course of action it led to a worse road with less attractive choices. As they made more and more wrong choices, the roads got worse and so did the options available to them.

Mary and Tommy are invented characters to illustrate a point but they are typical of many young people who get into trouble slowly. The sad part is that most of those who do keep making unfortunate choices refuse to take any personal responsibility at all. They blame the "system", "other people" or might shrug it off with "that's just my luck". As you can see, luck had very little to do with it.

Notice we said "very little" to do with it because luck did play a part. Neither Mary nor Tommy had anybody to teach them they were responsible for their lives or to explain the dangers of getting into debt or being influenced by bad company.

As Brian Tracy pointed out in his audio recording *The Psychology of Success,* the difference between winners and losers is that the losers believe that anything good that happens to them is a lucky break and blame everything bad that happens on somebody or something else. As a result, they never take responsibility for what happens in their lives and forever deny themselves the chance to learn.

In contrast, the winners take full credit for their successes and treat their failures as a learning experience.

The above is probably obvious when you think about it. If so, why do so many people fail to take control of their lives?

People fail to take control of their lives because:
- They don't believe they have the ability.
- They don't want to put in the effort.
- They have been conditioned to believe they are victims.
- They don't know how to get started.

We'll now think about each of these in turn and discuss ways to overcome them in the light of what we have read so far.

NO FAITH IN YOUR ABILITY

This is caused by a faulty self-concept that is probably the result of a previous failure pattern created by past failures in your life, or because you have always been too frightened to try anything. It can also be caused by comparing yourself to others in an unfavourable light. You may have noticed that people tend to compare their worst feature to a world figure's best feature. For example, they compare their looks to a Hollywood movie star's looks and their sporting skills to that of an international champion.

A good way to start is to stop comparing yourself with others. Then concentrate on becoming an authority on something.

The range of subjects is limitless, as the sole aim of the exercise is for you to prove to yourself you have the ability to do it. It could be skating, knowing the history of the local football team, rock music, cooking pikelets, growing roses, making model aeroplanes, or, if you are a junior in an office, knowing how to save postage. That last one might not sound too exciting, but the postage rates are confusing and nothing will get you noticed quicker than coming up with ways to save your boss money.

Once you become an "expert" in your chosen subject, and also practise the techniques described in the chapter on self-concept, you will find that your faith in yourself will grow as you start to enjoy a small measure of self-esteem.

NOT WANTING TO PUT IN THE EFFORT

Often it has been said that winners are those who do what losers are unwilling to do. The cold reality is that making the effort is one of the factors that sets the winners apart. By now you should be aware that everything has a price but finally the rewards that come from that price far outweigh it. Do you remember Emerson's Law of Compensation from the last chapter?

From my observations, it is lack of motivation, not laziness, that inflicts so many. Why do some people who have to drag themselves to work for five days of the week leap out of bed at 4am to go fishing on Sunday morning? Where does the energy come from to party all night?

The way to overcome the lack of enthusiasm for work is to find a job you enjoy because when you have done that you have turned your work into a hobby.

Here's something to think about:

- Thomas Edison used to work 18 hours a day but once remarked, "I never did a day's work in my life. It was all fun."
- Dale Carnegie, author of one of the most acclaimed books of all time, *How to Win Friends and Influence People,* said, "Nobody is to be pitied as much as the person who gets nothing out of his job but his pay."
- Confucius, a famous Chinese philosopher born in 551BC, said, "If you enjoy what you do, you'll never work another day in your life."

The best way to find a job you enjoy is to keep learning and finding new experiences to try until you find your niche. Noel found he had triple the energy when he started his own business for, at last, the responsibilities and the rewards were his. And don't be too disheartened by all the pressure that our education systems can put on us. Although you should study hard to create as many options for you as possible, it's not the end of the world if you don't do as well as you'd hoped on an assignment or an exam. But think about developing the habit of commitment so you can apply it to other areas of your life.

James says...

These days there is so much pressure on young people to choose a career path in their early teens and stick to it. As you've just read, if you don't enjoy what you're doing then you're very unlikely to "give it your all" or stick with it over the long term. When you're young, focus more on developing the habits, rather than a specific career, and eventually you'll find yourself attracted to something you enjoy instead of something you were forced to choose.

BAD CONDITIONING

If you have come from a family background where it is the normal practice to blame everybody else for what goes wrong, you will have to do some serious thinking. It is unlikely you will change the views of the older members of the family so you will have to compensate for their negative input with positive material from other sources.

Try to find some positive people to mix with and, if possible, start (or join) a mastermind group. The material listed at the back of this book will help and, as you read and understand more, you will be able to recognise any negative input from those close to you for what it is.

NOT KNOWING HOW TO GET STARTED

Maybe you don't know how to start. Maybe you have so many other things on your plate that you can't make the time to start. Or maybe you're just the victim of good old procrastination. Whatever it is, you should understand that starting any project is often difficult. The hardest part of writing a book is preparing the chapter outlines. Rick Everingham, the painter, believes that nothing is more difficult than staring at a blank canvas. The great Russian author Fyodor Dostoevsky said, "Taking a new step, uttering a new word, is what people fear most." The Scottish writer Samuel Smiles believed, "The reason why so little is done is generally because so little is attempted."

You start by setting practical and simple goals. Then you use the "Salami Technique" (which we mentioned in the chapter on goal setting) to make some steady progress. Once you make that first step, the rest will fall into place.

It can be difficult to move out of your comfort zone and start to accept full responsibility for your actions. However, only by doing this can you take charge of your life and direct it where you want to go. Your future is safer in your hands than in the

hands of somebody else, and infinitely more fulfilling.

MAKING YOUR MONEY WORK

The previous chapters have focused on ways that
you can realise your potential and make yourself
more valuable in the marketplace. This in turn will
improve your income; after all, it's the income
stream that you receive during your working life
that is the foundation for the wealth you will accumulate. However, all the income in the world is of
no long-term benefit to you unless you put some of
it away. How does a person earning $10,000 a week
go broke? Simple. Spend $11,000 a week.

A detailed blueprint for turning your income into
assets is given in Noel's book *Making Money Made
Simple* and this should be the next book you read
after you finish this one. Therefore, in the chapters
that follow we will give you a brief overview to
prepare you for more detailed information when you
get to *Making Money Made Simple.*

Noel learnt two great lessons about money in
his working life but unfortunately he was nearly 40
when he stumbled across them. You have the chance
to start much earlier. These lessons are the two
fundamental principles of wealth building and if you
follow them it's hard to go wrong. The first is "how
little things add up", the second is what we call "the
Guaranteed Secret of Wealth". We'll discuss that
next.

The vault:

- Your life is in **your** hands.
- Where you will be in the future depends on the choices you make from now on.
- Take responsibility and ownership for everything that happens in your life.
- There's not much to gain from comparing yourself with others.
- Making the effort is one of the factors that sets the winners apart.
- Keep learning and finding new experiences to try until you find your niche.
- Get out of your comfort zone.

17

THE REALITYOF MONEY

If only God would give me some clear sign; like making a large deposit in my name in a Swiss bank.

Woody Allen

In this chapter we will explain what money is and what it can—and can't—do for you.

We live in a rich country where opportunities abound and where most people who are young now will earn millions of dollars before they stop work. Yet, most of them will spend all their lives worrying about money and retire with nothing more than a house and a few thousand dollars in the bank.

The knowledge you have gained, and are gaining, will set you apart from "most people". When you have finished this book, you should be able to work towards a goal of complete financial security if you so desire. In the next few chapters we will show you how to make money, how to spend it and how to accumulate it. Like surfing, it's important to practise on the beach before you hit the waves so you can get the little things right. You don't want to jump right in and wipeout on your first investment. That's why everything before this chapter is so important—we've been building the fundamentals so that you are ready to tackle the more detailed chapters.

Before money was around, people used the barter system. You shod my horse and I gave you some eggs and butter in return. That was a cumbersome process and people found that coins were simpler as they solved such obvious problems as trying to barter a bale of hay for half a horse. The wealthier ones hoarded gold, which was usually left at the goldsmith's for safe keeping. The goldsmith gave out receipts for each bar of gold and if you needed some gold to pay a debt you went to the goldsmith, handed over your receipt, withdrew the required amount of gold and delivered it to your creditor in payment.

This was also cumbersome and the citizens found it was easier to use the receipts themselves as a means of exchange. If I owed you two bars of gold, I simply signed two of my receipts over to you. This entitled you to withdraw two of my bars of gold from the goldsmith when you wished. After a time, the receipts themselves started to act as money and eventually few holders bothered to go to the goldsmith to withdraw the physical gold.

As civilisation grew and business became more complex, banks gradually took over from the goldsmiths and finally receipts issued by banks took over from the goldsmith's receipts. Then the banks started to issue their own "banknotes" (a "note" is a term for a loan document) because it was more convenient for their customers to have money in various denominations.

However, banks are not immune from disaster and occasionally a note-issuing bank would go broke and cause huge losses to those unfortunate people who held its notes issued. One by one the government of each country took over the issuing of money and the banks gave up doing it.

As you can see, the need for convenience changed the system and it is still changing today. We now live in a society where many people hardly see money at all. Their pay goes direct into their account and they withdraw it by debit card or by writing cheques. Despite the change in the method of completing a transaction, the essential nature of money has not changed—it is a means of exchange. It enables us to exchange our goods and services for the goods and services of others.

Unfortunately, far too many people focus solely on the money side of their life. The Bible says, "For we brought nothing into this world, and it is certain we can carry nothing out ... The love of money is the root of all evil."[24] Money cannot buy happiness, health, fine weather, contentment or good relationships, and we doubt if there are many wealthy old people who would not give up all of their wealth in exchange for being young again.

---

24 1 Timothy ch.6

However, make no mistake about it—money is important in the areas where it works. These include providing a home, a good education, top health care, the opportunity to help others, clothes and the chance to experience the excitement of travel. What we like about money is that it enables you to make more choices in your life, choices that are based on what you want to do, not what you have to do.

Noel and his wife Geraldine travel a lot and have eaten occasionally at restaurants that are recognised as the finest in the world. They have done it for the experience but are just as happy eating in cheap sidewalk restaurants where the food is a quarter of the price and nobody minds if you strike up a conversation with the people at the next table to practise the language. The point is that having money allows them a genuine choice—if they eat at sidewalk restaurants it is because they prefer to be there.

Now let's consider a few basics.

MONEY WON'T MAKE YOU HAPPY

Most of us have dreamed of having millions of dollars in a foreign bank and spending life cruising around the world in yachts or going to fancy parties. If that's your goal, and you work hard and give up enough for it, you might even get there. However, in reality most of that stuff is dreamed up by Hollywood scriptwriters and, although the fancy mansions and the huge yachts do exist, there is plenty of evidence that the lifestyle does not equate to happiness. If you want proof, look up some biographies on the internet of the so-called "glamorous people".

It came as a shock to us to discover there was almost no connection between money and happiness. The happiest person we know is a 75-year-old woman who rents a small apartment and has less than $5,000 in the bank. She was well off once but a gambling husband lost it all and left her alone to bring up a large family. She has coped magnificently with such a personal tragedy and lives a happy and fulfilled life. In contrast, we know wealthy people who are often unhappy because they don't realise that enjoying what they have is more important than the amount of money they have. Above all, it is the ability to enjoy life that makes for real happiness.

However, there is a huge connection between being unhappy and having money troubles. It is no fun to watch your car being towed away because you failed to make the payments, to arrive home to find your power and phone have been cut off, or to lose your home because of interest rate rises.

Financial pressures have also been reported to destroy relationships. A 2008 study from *Relationships Australia* found that over 40% of people list "money troubles" as a major pressure on their relationship.

WHY ACCUMULATE MONEY?

Money is a medium that enables you to exchange your services for that of another. However, by itself, it is useless—if you are stranded in a burning hot desert, a suitcase full of money won't quench your thirst. What counts is what it can do for you. Having money to spend may make you feel good, it may provide a feeling of freedom or security and for many people it is even a way of keeping score.

Because you use money to pay for another's services, and you receive money by providing services, it follows that the amount of money you get depends on how much service you give. It's important to understand this.

We have stressed it is preferable to have control over your life. Even though money won't make you happy, building up a store of investment capital will provide financial security and enable you to have more choices in what you do. Think about the following:

(1)   When you have money saved up, you can pay cash for what you want instead of borrowing and paying interest. As most people pay hun-

dreds of thousands of dollars in interest over a lifetime, it follows that reducing the interest you pay gives you money available for more productive purposes. For example, if Sally is paying $300 a month in car repayments, and Anne has a car that is free of debt, Anne has $300 a month more spending money available.

(2) The investment capital you build provides opportunities for you. It is possible you will have a chance to start your own business at some stage in your life, which usually requires you to have some money to put towards it. Wouldn't it be a shame if you missed an exciting money-making opportunity just because you had neglected to build up some capital for that purpose?

(3) Building up money gives you confidence in your ability to generate income and accumulate wealth. Once you have this confidence, you know you can do it and you won't be frightened to invest some of your capital in riskier projects. Fear of loss has held many people back and it is true that, as you get older, you are less able to take large risks because you do not have the time to rebuild your wealth. If you are going to lose some money, it is better to do it when you are young. Wouldn't it be a tragedy to realise when you are old that you could have achieved your dreams, but fear of loss held you back and you didn't get around to having a go?

(4) Money gives you more freedom. Once you have
established a capital base, either by accumulating income-producing investments or by building
up a business, you can take a break from your
job to explore other areas in your life. Certainly
it takes time to get to that stage but it's a
wonderful feeling to be able to take a month off
to trek through the mountains or even to take
a morning off to attend one of your children's
sports days.

Now that you understand what money can, and
can't, do for you, we'll move to the principles of
building wealth.

The vault:

- Financial security means more choices in life.
- There is almost no connection between money and
  happiness. It is the ability to enjoy life that makes
  for real happiness.
- Generally, the amount of money you get depends
  on how much service you give.
- An adequate capital base allows you to avoid interest repayments.

18

HOW TO BE RICH!!!

However easy it may be to make money, it is the most difficult thing in the world to keep it.

P.T. Barnum

In this chapter we will teach you how to start building a fortune. It is done by the combination of slowly accumulating capital and letting the magic of compound interest work on it for you.

You have now read over half this book and your eyes should be starting to open. You know you can do more than you are presently doing to build on your potential, and that success, whatever it means in your case, is not a matter of chance—it requires discipline and work. Now it's time to let you in on the secrets of building wealth.

If you've skipped over the earlier chapters and opened straight to this page because you like the title, you've missed out on valuable lessons and we strongly encourage you to read from the beginning to maximise your wealth-building potential. It will be much easier for you to grow (and keep) your wealth if you apply the principles we've discussed so far.

Like the other principles in this book, the secrets of wealth accumulation are not difficult nor are they hard to understand—it's purely a matter of getting into the habit of applying them.

STEP ONE—MANAGE YOUR MONEY

The first key to becoming wealthy is to learn to manage your money effectively. Tens of thousands of people earn big money and are always broke because the money just slips through their fingers. Obviously earning a pile of dollars is meaningless if you spend it all, so any wealth-building plan depends on your grabbing hold of some of that money as it comes pouring in. Even though it's obvious "most people" don't do it.

There is a simple and effective tool (called a "budget") for managing your money. We'll tell you about it in the next chapter. If you don't have a budget you will have no idea where your money went. Worse still, you may end up wasting most of it.

STEP TWO—UNDERSTAND HOWSMALL THINGS ACCUMULATE

People seldom succeed or fail in one great earth-shattering event. Rather, it is the succession of small things done, or not done, that makes the difference. For example, Matt saves 10% of each pay and Stephen spends a little more than he gets each pay by buying all sorts of stuff and charging it to his credit card. That mightn't sound like much, but after two years Matt has $5,000 in the bank and Stephen is $5,000 in debt. They are now $10,000 apart and they are both just 21! Who would you rather be?

Sophie spends just one hour per day studying material that will improve her skills and increase her effectiveness at work, but Claire spends the same hour watching TV. It's only an hour a day, but after three years Sophie has given over 1,000 hours to study and has become a leader in her field. Claire is left wondering why Sophie is now so successful and earning double what she earns.

In 1980 Noel showed home buyers how they could save thousands of dollars in home interest by making their payments weekly or fortnightly. For example, if a couple borrows $300,000 at 8%[25] the repayments over 30 years are $2,200 a month—a total of $792,000. The principal repaid is $300,000 and total interest is $492,000. Just by changing the repayments to $1,100 a fortnight, the term drops by six years and the total repayments fall to $136,400. Back in 1980 the banks all laughed at the idea but now most of them are advertising it. Better still, most homebuyers are doing it and speeding up their wealth creation process as well.

It seems like witchcraft but it's really simple if you think about it. There are 12 calendar months in a year but 26 fortnights—by making the payments fortnightly you pay back an extra $183 a month without realising

---

[25] Interest rates chosen for the purposes of the example may not reflect rates currently applicable.

it. Because of the magic of compound interest, discussed soon, this extra $183 a month makes a massive difference.

Notice one important factor. Most of the borrowers who are using this new system to save tens of thousands of dollars never had a cent to spare when they were paying monthly. They probably still haven't got a cent to spare. Nevertheless, by changing the payment frequency, they end up paying back an extra $183 a month or $2,196 a year.

STEP THREE—KNOW ABOUTTHE BOTTOM LINE

The "bottom line" is an accounting term that refers to a company's profit. In simple terms, a profit and loss account looks like this:

Gross business income	$500 000
Cost of running the business	$450 000
Net profit	$50 000

Note: "Gross business income" is the total income before taking taxes or deductions into account.

As you can clearly see, the term "bottom line" refers to the net profit because that's where it is placed when the financial statements are drawn up.

Now think about your own little profit and loss account.

Income after tax	$40 000
Costs of your lifestyle	$38 000
Amount left over for wealth creation	$2 000

The term "costs of your lifestyle" includes food, clothes, rent, loan repayments, entertainment, holidays and fares—all the items on which most people spend their money. Notice that, while they are expenses you often can't avoid, they are all consumed and have no lasting value. Therefore they are not available for creating wealth. You build wealth with the money you have over.

Imagine what would happen if you could increase your net income by 10% without increasing the costs of your lifestyle. Then your personal profit and loss account would read:

Income after tax	$44 000
Costs of your lifestyle	$38 000
Amount left over for wealth creation	$6 000

You have just gained a 300% increase on the amount you have left for wealth creation by increasing your net income by 10%. Isn't that a perfect example of the law of sowing and reaping? You always reap much more than you sow.

Perhaps that sounded obvious but now re-read the section above slowly and stop and think about it. It will change your life forever if you truly understand it. We have just taught you one of the most powerful secrets of wealth in the world—increasing your income without increasing your costs.

What would "most people" do? Every time they increase their income, they also increase their living costs. As the British humorist Parkinson put it,

"Expenditure rises to meet income."[26] Consequently, "most people" regard an increase in pay of $4,000 as an excuse to go on a spending spree. It would never occur to them that they had just missed the opportunity to treble their investment capital. As a result, they go through life broke and will continue to blame "the system".

STEP FOUR—MINIMISE BORROWINGFOR DEPRECIATING ITEMS

A major difference between financial winners and financial losers is that the winners borrow for items such as houses that gain in value, and the losers borrow for items such as furniture that drop in value. Resist the temptation to start buying goods on credit cards, avoid hire purchase and personal loans and, if possible, delay buying a car if you have to borrow for it. Use the family car, or public transport, for as long as possible.

---

[26] Parkinson, C.N. The Law and the Profits (1960) Chapter 1.

STEP FIVE—APPRECIATE THE IMPORTANCE OF INCREASING YOUR INCOME STREAM

Think of financial independence as a destination and the assets you accumulate along the way as the vehicle to get you there. The income you earn is the fuel that drives the vehicle—the more you can earn, the faster the trip will be—provided you use the income for wealth creation and not for consumer spending.

Unfortunately "most people" seem to believe the more you make, the more tax you pay, and therefore it is not worthwhile making the effort. Deep down they are probably too lazy to stretch themselves to provide the extra service to make the extra money. It's a stupid way to think, whatever their reasoning. There are many legal devices that can minimise tax, particularly if you have your own business or have investments.

STEP SIX—USE YOUR INCOME TO ACQUIRE ASSETS

You now know the importance of putting money aside for wealth creation. It can be done in two ways:
- By saving the money you have left over after paying your tax and your living expenses, or
- By using tax-effective borrowing.

Tax-effective borrowing means borrowing to buy assets that produce income. For example, an investor may buy shares or property worth $300,000 with a loan of $250,000. Suppose the returns (through dividends or rents) from that asset are $12,000 a year after all costs (including interest) have been paid. If the interest rate is 8%,[27] the interest will be $20,000 so the investor will be $8,000 short. The good news is that this shortfall can be claimed as a tax deduction so if you are in the 40% tax bracket, the tax department will be paying 40% of the shortfall for you.

We call this technique "negative gearing" and full details are given in *Making Money Made Simple.* We recommend it only after you have bought the home in which you live and substantially reduced the mortgage but we are mentioning it here to show you why it is so important to increase your income. When you have built up a substantial equity in that first home you will have both the asset base and the income stream to speed you along.

THE FORMULA

(1) To build wealth, you first have to produce income. You do this by improving your skills.

---

[27] Interest rates chosen for the purposes of the example may not reflect rates currently applicable.

(2)   Don't spend all you earn. Make sure you keep some to invest. It's your money, so why give it to someone else?

(3)   As your investment capital grows, it too will produce income. Now you have two sources of income—from your assets and from your work.

(4)   As your assets grow, use them, plus the money they are making for you, to buy more income-producing assets.

Naturally it takes time, particularly in the early stages, but you will discover in the next chapters that the process gets faster and faster as time goes by. But it will never start unless you earn money and keep some of it to invest.

The vault:

- The secrets of wealth accumulation are not difficult. It's purely a matter of getting into the habit of applying them.
- Learn to manage your money effectively.
- It is the succession of small things done, or not done, that makes the difference.
- Learn how to increase your income without increasing the costs.
- Borrow for items that appreciate in value, not the other way around.
- Don't spend all you earn. It's your money, why give it to someone else?
- Cultivate multiple sources of income to boost your wealth.

19

BUDGETING

The structure ... will automatically provide the pattern for the action which follows.

Donald Curtis

This chapter will teach you the importance of having a system to keep your finances on track and to prevent you frittering your money away.

The early chapters in this book concentrated on helping you improve the way you manage yourself to ensure you develop your personal potential. The next few chapters will show you how to manage your money so you get the best out it. There is little doubt you will earn a higher than average income if you follow the principles in this book but there is not much to be gained by having a high income if you waste every cent of it. The solution is to form the habit of managing your money properly.

First, you have to understand what is really meant by a budget. It's explained in full in *Making Money Made Simple* and you can study it in detail when you read that book. In this chapter we'll just give you the basics.

THE FIRST PAY CHEQUE

Let's start with the fundamentals and imagine you have found your first job, are still living at home, and have just received your first pay packet. Congratulate yourself, you have taken a vital step to independence by earning some money of your own. You have just turned on a tap from which millions of dollars are going to gush in your lifetime—it's like finding an oil well in your backyard that will support you for life. You are now on the road to wealth, provided you develop a few simple habits.

This may be a fitting time to reflect once more that "most people" never get to learn about these habits, much less practise them. They will also earn millions of dollars in their working life, but will be constantly broke and will finish up with their hands stretched out for the welfare cheque. The techniques in this book will give you the opportunity to live differently if you start to practise them.

Because you are young, the first pay cheque probably won't be a big one and the natural reaction is to say to yourself, "I'll spend all of this but when I start to earn big money I'll put a plan in place to manage my money properly and make it grow." If you start thinking like that you will join "most people" who continually say, "If I win the Lotto I'll start to take care of my money." It's an irony because, if they had always taken care of their money, they wouldn't be worried about winning the Lotto today. They're the same people who say "If I had a good body I'd look after it."

Do you see, now, how it all works together? Life's losers say they will go the extra mile at work **after** they get the promotion, and manage their money properly **after** they become wealthy. Unfortunately, for them, life doesn't work like that.

It's not the money that counts, it's the habit. Therefore, you should look upon that first money you earn as giving you an opportunity to start developing good habits that will give you an edge on everybody else.

The major goal is to get into the habit of living within your means, something "most people" never do. When people spend even just a little more than they earn, they have to borrow small amounts to get by. This way of going into debt is like contracting a slow creeping disease. It is so important that we have devoted two chapters to it in this book.

Your other goal should be to save a portion of each pay. How much? If you are living at home, probably 20% of your net pay is reasonable. It is easier to save a larger part of your income while you are living at home and can get cheap board and perhaps the use of the family car.

Now we know that saving $50 a week out of a wage of $250 will seem like chicken feed and probably after a few weeks you'll look at your bank balance of a few hundred dollars and wonder if such small amounts of savings are worth worrying about.

Let's repeat the secret—it's not the money, it's the habit. Most of your peers will save nothing, or worse still, will already be starting to acquire the habit of depending on credit cards. By saving 20% of your take home pay and living within your means, you will put a habit in place that will virtually guarantee you will be one of the few people who become wealthy.

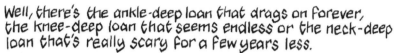

However, you have to beware of the power of human nature—we tend to spend whatever we get. Ask around and you will find that almost all your friends, and their parents and their friends, have trouble living on their incomes even though they all have different incomes.

The trick is to have the 20% you wish to save deducted from your salary and paid straight to a special account with your bank, building society or credit union. If you do that, and put money away in another account for essential expenses, you can spend the rest on clothes, holidays, entertainment, restaurants and having fun with a clear conscience.

This is also a good time to practise your newly acquired knowledge of setting goals. Why not plan to have a special holiday in 12 months time? Work out the cost of it, open a special holiday account, and put in part of the cost each week. Start that habit now and you are assured of good holidays for the rest of your life.

Now you understand the theory of budgeting, let's move to the practical part and prepare one. It is simply a matter of preparing a schedule that lists your income followed by the items on which you wish to spend your money. We have shown a sample budget and you will notice the items are listed in order of priority, with "savings" at the top of the list and all the "fun" things at the bottom.

The "fun" items, such as entertainment and travel, are at the bottom because at a pinch you can do without them. They are not as important to your future as savings, fares and food. Unfortunately "most people" spend on the fun things first and find there is never anything left over for savings. Then they promise to start "next week" which of course never comes.

SPECIMEN BUDGET

Income after tax $250
ESSENTIAL ITEMS
Savings a/c $150
Holiday a/c 30
Fares 30
Grooming 10
Board 20
Self-Education Exps 10
Total essential items $150
BALANCE REMAINING FOR
Clothes
Movies
Restaurants
Entertainment
Etc, etc, etc. $100

After just 12 months there will be over $2,600 in the investment savings account and around $1,600 in the holiday account when interest is credited. Can you imagine how good it will feel to know you have saved over $4,000 in your first year of working?

If you understand the power of budgeting, you will quickly establish yourself as a person who can manage money and who can set and achieve goals. The result will be more than a future free of financial problems—it will almost surely mean a great sense of wellbeing and self-esteem.

The vault:

- It's not the money that counts, it's the habit.
- Beware of the power of human nature—we tend to spend whatever we get.
- Prioritise your expenses to identify areas where you can save money.

20

UNDERSTANDING INTEREST

Put each coin to labouring that it may reproduce its kind even as the flocks of the field and help bring to thee income, a stream of wealth that shall flow constantly into thy purse. [28]

George M. Clason

"Interest" will make you or break you. Therefore, if you are going to get ahead in this world you will need to understand the concept of interest and use it to build your wealth. However, interest is like fire—a good servant but a bad master. In this chapter you will learn how to make it work to your advantage and how to keep away from the dangers.

A good way to define interest is "the price paid by somebody who borrows money to somebody who lends it".

There are three areas in which people invest the bulk of their money. In each case the investment gives the person with the money a benefit. The three areas are:

---

28 Clason, George. The Richest Man in Babylon (1985:33) Bantam.

(1) Money lent out to institutions such as banks, finance companies, building societies and credit unions who, in turn, lend it to people who wish to borrow money. The borrowers pay interest in return for the use of the money.

(2) Real estate, which gives you free shelter if it is your own home, or provides you with income by way of rent if you are a landlord.

(3) Shares in companies. The shares usually provide the investor with a share of the profits in the company by paying profits out as "dividends".

As you can see, if you have money to invest it can be made to give you benefits. These benefits may be more income (through interest, rent and dividends), or in the form of free accommodation (if you buy a house). However, if you are receiving money, there must be somebody else paying it out. Obviously it makes sense to be getting it **in** rather than paying it **out.** To help you understand this, we'll follow a money trail to show you how it all comes together.

HOW TO MAKE INTEREST WORK FOR YOU

Ted and Alice are retired and have over $350,000 in cash. They "deposit" the money in an account at the XYZ Bank and receive interest at the rate of 7%* per annum. This means that every year the bank pays Ted and Alice $24,500 for the privilege of being able to use their money.

Lachlan and Katie are a young couple who have always wanted a home of their own. They have been saving as fast as they can for this home and have accumulated $50,000 in the XYZ Bank. It is paying them 7%* interest as well. But there is a problem. They have discovered the amount they can save, even with the benefit of the interest the bank is paying them, is not increasing as quickly as the growth in house prices. The only way they can solve the problem is to use somebody else's money to help them buy the house.

The house they want is now selling for $400,000. After some serious discussion, they decide to take the plunge and borrow $350,000 from the bank to use to buy the house.

They pay the bank 8.5%[29] for the use of the money, although you could say they are using Ted and Alice's money with the bank acting as the go-between.

Everybody is doing well out of the deal. The retired couple are gaining interest for allowing somebody else to use their money, and the young couple now have a house even if it does have a big mortgage. The bank is doing well too—it is paying Ted and Alice $24,500 for the use of the money and collecting $29,750 from Lachlan and Katie. The profit of $5,250 is used to pay the costs of running the bank, such as staff wages

---

[29] Interest rates chosen for the purposes of the example may not reflect rates currently applicable.

and rent, and a substantial part of what is leftover will be paid to the bank's shareholders as dividends.

You can see now the concept of interest has enabled Ted and Alice to earn money to live on in retirement and it has also helped Lachlan and Katie to buy a house. It's a win/win situation.

Notice another important point. The only reason Lachlan and Katie borrowed the money was to enable them to buy the house today instead of waiting for a date in the future when the house might cost more. The interest they pay is the price of doing this, but how large a price is now up to them. It is not like buying a Big Mac where you know the price when you walk into McDonald's. They will continue to pay interest to the bank until the entire loan is paid back.

A SMART WAY TO INVEST MONEY

If Lachlan and Katie choose to pay it back over a long term, say 30 years, they will have to repay $2,691 a month. Because of the long term of the loan, the repayments in the early years are mainly interest only. In fact, in the first month the bank keeps $2,479 of that $2,691 payment for interest, which leaves only $212 a month for reducing the loan balance. Even after five years they still owe $334,000 and the bank is taking $2,366 interest from each monthly payment, and a mere $325 is coming off the loan balance.

If they had kept repaying $2,691 a month for 30 long years, Lachlan and Katie would have paid back $619,000 interest as well as the original sum of $350,000—a total of $969,000. The price of borrowing the money to enable them to buy that house today has been over half a million dollars. That's huge!!

There is more bad news. As you learn more about investment, you will discover that interest paid on a loan for your own home is not allowed as a tax deduction. Therefore, you make your housing repayments from that part of your income that is left after tax has come out. These remaining dollars are called "after tax dollars". Lachlan and Katie would have to earn over $1,058,000 just to produce the after tax dollars to pay that interest bill of $619,000.

Luckily Lachlan and Katie are educated borrowers. They had read Noel's books, were aware of the way interest worked, and had decided to take control of the situation by using all their efforts to pay off the loan quickly. They both worked and repayments of $4,000 a month were within their capacity. That extra payment of $1,309 a month requires total additional repayments of almost $78,540 over the first seven years of the loan, but after those seven years of struggle the debt is down to just $176,000.

Their loan is now down to a level where it can be handled easily on one income, but if they maintained repayments of $4,000 a month the loan would be repaid in 11 years with just $198,000 of interest.

The extra payments saved them $421,000 of after tax dollars in interest. That's the equivalent of their earning an extra $716,000 of pre tax dollars!! Can you think of an easier way to earn $716,000?

A SILLY WAY TO SPEND INTEREST

Lachlan and Katie saved thousands of dollars in interest because they were smart enough to invest in an asset that will grow in value and because they knew how much they could save by paying their loan back quickly.

Tom and Jess took a different approach. They decided to buy a car. They had never been savers so took out a loan of $40,000 to cover the entire purchase price. They decided to go for the longest term to keep the repayments down to a level that would allow them plenty of money left over to spend on clothes, nights out and travel. They let the car dealer arrange the finance and found themselves borrowing

$40,000 over five years at 17%.[30] The monthly repayment came to $994 and they paid back a total of $59,650 over the five years. The interest bill alone amounted to $19,650 much of which could have been avoided if they had saved a large deposit and paid the loan back over a shorter term.

HOW DELAY AFFECTS INTEREST

If you are a borrower, the three factors that influence the total interest you pay are:
- The amount borrowed
- The interest rate, and
- The amount you repay each year.

You will learn in the next chapter (on compound interest) about the importance of starting early, but you should also understand that a few years delay in buying an item that is growing in value could cost you dearly.

For example, when she was 25, Amanda bought a home unit for $250,000 with a $40,000 deposit. She borrowed $210,000 and paid it back over 15 years at $2,068 a month. By her 40th birthday the unit was paid off. Her total repayments (principal and interest) were $372,240.

Peter waited till he was 30 and then paid $300,000 for a similar property because prices had risen. He

---

[30] Interest rates chosen for the purposes of the example may not reflect rates currently applicable.

also put down $40,000 deposit, but had to repay $2,256 a month because he borrowed $260,000. The term of the loan was 20 years and his total repayments were over $541,000.

Let's now assume that Amanda, having paid off her unit, now invests $2,256 a month—the same amount that Peter is paying on his mortgage. Contrast where the pair of them will be at age 50. Amanda not only has a mortgage-free home but may also have accumulated over $460,000 from her investments. Peter, however, will be making his final home payment.

WHAT INTEREST DOES

Interest is the price you pay to get some money to use today if you are short of money. You should ask yourself: "Is it worth paying a price to have spending power available now?" Only you can answer that question but you will find most people borrow money for one of four reasons:

(1) They want to buy an expensive asset (such as a house) and believe it is better to buy now before prices go up.

(2) They need the use of a depreciating asset (such as a washing machine, furniture or a car) now and don't have the money available.

(3) They want to indulge themselves with a holiday or big-screen TV but don't have any available savings.

(4) They have pressing expenses (such as the electricity bill) to pay but have no money put aside because of never managing their money properly. They will suffer unpleasant consequences if the money is not found somehow.

As these topics are covered in detail in *Making Money Made Simple* we will not explore them in detail here. Notice you could argue a case that it is acceptable to borrow for the first two reasons. However, if anybody has to borrow for the last two reasons it is obvious they are not practising budgeting or that they suffer from a lack of control.

HOW INTEREST CAN HELP YOU

Once you have money saved up, you can invest it and receive interest on it. This means you have increased your income because you now have interest coming in, as well as the other income from your work—you've cultivated multiple sources of income. In the next chapter you will see how the miracle of compound interest can make your savings grow at a faster and faster rate.

If you have to spend money on interest, one of the best ways to become wealthy is to buy real estate. Probably the real estate you know best is the house or unit in which you live. If your parents have been following Noel's advice about paying off the loan on the property quickly, they may now own the property without any mortgage.

Stop and think about the benefits of that for a second.

No loan repayments to make, no rent to pay and no fear of being kicked out in the street if the landlord decides to sell the property. That's what we call a feeling of security.

However, even if they own the house now with no mortgage, it is highly likely they borrowed money when they bought it originally. They may have been paying rent of $400 a week and discovered this was nearly as much as the repayments on a home. They decided to buy a place of their own, instead of being at the mercy of landlords for the rest of their life. They had to make an important decision—do they keep on paying rent and try to save the full price of a house, or do they use the money they have as part payment for the house and borrow money for the balance? Luckily for you they took the plunge and bought the house.

You should now appreciate that interest is the price you pay to spend money you don't have. Once you start to borrow, you are promising to pay a part of your future income to another person who is the source of the money that has been lent to you. Whether the price is justified is a matter only you can decide.

The vault:

- Interest is the price you pay to spend money you don't have.
- If you are a borrower, the three factors that influence the total interest you pay are the amount borrowed, the interest rate and the amount you repay each year.

21

COMPOUND INTEREST

Do not despise the bottom rungs in the ascent to greatness.

Publilius Syrus

Get ready—in this chapter you will have a mathematics lesson. Don't let the topic scare you off because it may well be the most profitable maths lesson you have ever had.

Financial textbooks often refer to the "magic" of compound interest because what happens when you use it appears to be truly miraculous. You read in a previous chapter that interest is a fee that is paid to you for the hire of your money, and paid by you when you want to hire somebody else's money. The interest is usually paid by the borrower to the lender on a regular basis. Generally this is monthly, but it may be quarterly or even yearly.

However, there is another way for a lender to receive interest—it may be added to the principal (the amount already owing) and left to grow. This is called compounding the interest because the principal is then bigger as a result of the compounded interest. Do you notice how, when this happens, the borrower is paying interest on interest? This interest on the interest may also be compounded and when the next lot of interest is due it is also added to the principal and the compounded interest. Now the poor old borrower is paying interest on interest on interest.

This is how it works:

Loan $10,000
Interest rate 10%

Interest is due each year and is compounded by being added to the principal.

Year 1

Original sum borrowed	$10 000
Interest for first year	$1 000
Balance owing end of Year 1	$11 000

Year 2

Opening balance	$11 000
Interest for second year	$1 100
Balance end of Year 2	$12 100

Year 3

Opening balance	$12 100
Interest for third year	$1 210
Balance end of Year 3	$13 210

That all looks innocent, doesn't it? It may, until you analyse the figures. After just three

years, the borrowers owe 32% more than they originally borrowed. Moreover, the interest bill in the third
year is 21% more than the interest for the first year.
It's often been called "creeping into big trouble".

You can work out the effect of compound interest
by using the Rule of 72.[31] This miraculous little trick
works with any interest rate. Write down the number
72 and divide it by the interest rate. The answer is
the number of years for the amount you owe to
double. If we use 10% from the example above, it
looks like:

$$\frac{72}{10\%} = 7.2 \text{ years}$$

Using the Rule of 72 we have now calculated that
$10,000 would double in just over seven years if the
interest was allowed to compound instead of being
paid to the lender at regular intervals. Therefore, after
7.2 years the borrowers would owe $20,000 instead
of the $10,000 they borrowed at the start.

Let's go a step further and imagine we left the
money untouched for another seven years. The debt
would double again. Now the hapless borrowers would
owe $40,000. That's right—in just 14 years, because
of compound interest, the borrowers would owe four
times what they borrowed in the first place. Leave

---

[31]   Full details of the Rule of 72 are in Making Money Made
       Simple.

this compounding process for another seven years and the debt is $80,000.

Think about that for a minute.

The $10,000 has grown to $80,000 in just 21 years. It has increased by 800%. That's an average of 38% each year on the original sum.

Notice how compounding starts slowly, but gets faster and faster and faster. It is just like an avalanche that may start with a few stones sliding down a mountain and picks up speed and size as the stones collect rocks. These rocks in turn collect huge boulders until the avalanche is like a torrent of stone pounding down the slope.

"How does this affect me?" you may be thinking. It affects you in two ways. Once you understand the principles of compound interest, you can avoid being trapped into dangerous levels of debt. **And** you can also use the knowledge to slowly build a fortune. This is because it can speed up the rate at which your money grows. For example, in the chapter about baby James and the Magic Train in *More Money with Noel Whittaker* Noel tells how an investment of $2.73 a day could grow at such at rate that when James has his 26th birthday his portfolio would be worth almost $109,000 and it could be growing at $210 a week due to a combination of capital growth and dividends.[32]

---

[32]   These figures are calculated using Noel Whittaker's Wealth Creator and are based on an investment of $2.73 a day

The problem for "most people" who try to build wealth through compounding is that the compounding process starts slowly and they tire of it before it has had a chance to work. Then they cash in the investment and blow the money on a holiday or a car.

The following example will show you how your money can grow. Imagine you put $10,000 into an investment that paid you a return of 10% compounded. The end of year values would be:

End of Year 1	11 047
End of Year 5	16 453
End of Year 10	27 070
End of Year 15	44 539
End of Year 20	73 281
End of Year 25	120 589
End of Year 30	198 374
End of Year 35	326 387
End of Year 40	537 007

Notice how the growth for the first five years is only $6,453 in the second five years $10,617, yet in the last five years $210,620. There is almost as much growth in those last five years as there was in the first 30 years.

This is why it is so important to start building your wealth at a young age.

---

into a fund that matches the All Ordinaries Accumulation Index.

In the example above, there is interest of only $6,453 in those first five years and you could rightly claim it's insignificant. However, a 35 year program would return $326,387, and a 40 year program would return $537,007. Putting off the wealth building program for five years could cost over $210,000.

ANOTHER SECRET OF WEALTH

Unfortunately, income tax can punch a hole in your plans because Australia has a progressive tax system; that is, the rate of tax rises as your income rises. However, when you buy an asset such as property or shares, any capital gain automatically is added to the asset value without any action on your part. As a result, the compounding process is automatic and no capital gains tax is payable until the asset is sold.

A clever way to wealth, which is used by most serious investors, is to borrow money for the asset and to pay the interest regularly instead of letting it compound. When they do this, the asset value should grow faster and faster because of the compounding effect.[33] At the same time, the debt will remain static and the investors' equity (the difference between the asset value and the loan) will grow.

Let's use some simple figures to illustrate the point. Imagine an investor bought an investment

---

[33] Naturally this assumes the asset will enjoy capital growth. If it falls in value the owner's loss is magnified.

property for $350,000 using a deposit of $50,000 in combination with an interest only loan of $300,000. The deposit is called the "investor's equity". If the interest on the loan was $21,000 a year and the net rents from the property were $21,000 a year, the investor could sit back and let the tenant pay the interest as the income was covering the outgoings. If the house doubled in value in 10 years, and the loan balance did not drop, the investor would then have a $700,000 house with a $300,000 loan. The initial equity of $50,000 has grown to $400,000 ($700,000 house value minus $300,000 loan=$400,000).

What has always fascinated us about compound interest is that it works in ways that seem totally illogical.

Think about two young people beginning separate investment programs for their retirement. The first starts putting $2,000 a year away at age 19 but stops at 26 to buy a home. The second does not start until age 26 but then invests, without fail, $2,000 a year till age 65.

Who do you think will end up with the largest sum of money (assuming a 10% rate of return)?

Strange, though it may seem, the winner is the first one who contributed only $14,000 but ended up with $945,000. The loser is the one who delayed and finished with $894,000 for a total investment of $80,000.

We hope this lesson on compound interest has got you fired up and ready to go. Don't forget that it takes time to work and that you need money to use it. Our next lesson will show you how to make that money.

The vault:

- Start building your wealth as early as possible.
- The Rule of 72 (72 divided by the interest rate) calculates the number of years it takes for the amount you owe to double.
- Understanding compound interest can help you avoid being trapped into dangerous levels of debt and can also help you to build a fortune.

22

THE GUARANTEED SECRET OF WEALTH

Being rich is having money; being wealthy is having time.

Margaret Bonnano

Noel says...

It hit me first in 1991—the country was still suffering the effects of the 1987 share crash, followed by the 1990 property crash, and many of us were starting to wonder if any investments were still worthwhile. And of course something very similar happened to investor sentiment throughout the banking troubles of 2007/2008 (sometimes called the "sub prime crisis") when a vast number of mortgage loans went bad in the United States and the resulting ripple effect hit banks and other financial services firms around the world.

Back in the early 1990s I started to think about what had worked for me and what had failed, and I suddenly saw this great truth. Our attitude to money is like our attitude to time—we *always find time to do the jobs we have to do but then find there is nothing left for anything else. We might not have time for exercise in the morning but we do have time for a shower. We may not have time to go to the gym but we do have time to go out partying with friends.*

Doesn't it follow that the only way to make sure we do the things we have to do is to prioritise them? Does that not lead to the logical conclusion that the only way to become wealthy is to make investing a priority? I called that "revelation" the Guaranteed Secret of Wealth.

While you might agree that it's important to make investment a priority, you may also feel that with all the calls on your income it's easy to overlook it (a "call" is any part of your life, good or bad, that requires short-term financial attention). This is what my Guaranteed Secret of Wealth is all about—making investment a priority and doing it in such a way that it happens automatically.

Remember we told you that up to 1980 or so everybody made their home loan repayments monthly. That was until Noel stirred up the banks by going on national TV and telling people they could save a fortune in interest if they made their payments weekly or fortnightly instead. All the banks scoffed at the idea. They claimed that, because the interest was charged monthly, paying weekly or fortnightly made no difference.

The banks had missed the point. It didn't have a thing to do with when the interest was charged.

It's worth revisiting the example we gave you in the Chapter 18. Think about a couple paying back $2,200 a month on a $300,000 housing loan over 30 years. They will almost certainly go through the following process—they will get paid, put aside the money for the loan repayments, spend the rest and arrive at next pay day broke.

Look at what happens when they move to fortnightly payments. They still get paid, put aside the money for the loan repayments, spend the rest and arrive at next pay day broke.

Nothing has changed. Or has it?

Now they are paying $1,100 a fortnight instead of $2,200 a month. But, there are 26 fortnights in a year and only 12 months. Annual payments have risen from $26,400 (12x$2,200) to $28,600 (26x$1,100) with the result that the loan term has dropped by seven years and they have saved over $137,000 in non-deductible interest.

What is different? Nothing, except that by using a smart strategy, they were compelled to pay an extra $40 a week off their home loan. Did they find the extra payments a burden? Not at all! Did it make a difference to their financial wellbeing? A massive difference! $137,000 in interest saved, and the loan paid off seven years earlier.

That's the first principle: "You don't miss what you don't get".

Surely it follows that if you have your investment money deducted automatically you won't miss it either. All banks nowadays have internet banking facilities in place so you can easily manage your finances online. Create a special savings account and, as soon as you can, transfer the amount you would like to save for a special purchase like the "bicycle" we discussed earlier (your bicycle might be a car, a holiday or even a house). It's an easy lesson to learn when you see what happens to savings that are left in your everyday account—they get squandered on everyday items that you won't even be able to remember at the end of the month.

Now let's think about another real-life situation. Ten people go out to dinner at a fancy restaurant and the bill comes to $1,000. One member of the party puts the entire $1,000 on her credit card and the other people give her $100 each. She goes home with a $1,000 debit on her credit card and an extra $900 in her wallet. That's fair, isn't it? What do you think will be the situation in four weeks time when the credit card statement with the $1,000 restaurant bill on it comes in? Do you really think she'll still have that $900 in her pocket? Chances are it has been frittered away on everyday items that were of no long-term use.

That's the second principle: "Money in your wallet just goes."

A wonderful illustration of the Guaranteed Secret of Wealth at work is the behaviour of borrowers in the late 1980s when housing interest rates jumped. Interest rates went to record levels and, naturally, mortgage repayments went up too. This stretched the budgets of many households, but less than 1% of people lost their homes. The rest managed to cope with the burden of the extra payments, and the smart ones kept up the higher payments when rates inevitably fell again.

Do you know why most people didn't let the bank foreclose on their mortgages? Because they knew the importance of keeping the family home. It is their shelter and the focus of family life, and it is also something that is there right now. Of course, the loss of it would cause a family trauma.

Saving for the future is just as important—the problem is that it is not immediate. Delay the investment program for a week, a month or even three years, and the sky won't fall in.

But, all of a sudden, age 45 comes around, and you start to think of retirement as something that may be just 120 months away. The moment you do the calculations you face the unpleasant truth that you have let time get away from you. Now it's a matter of starting a massive savings program for the next 10 years, when life was just starting to get a bit easier, or delaying that long-awaited retirement until age 60 or 65. All because you didn't get around to practising the Guaranteed Secret of Wealth.

Now that you understand the way the Guaranteed Secret of Wealth works, find ways to put it into practice. For example, simply arrange internet banking facilities so you can save the money you want to. As soon as it enters your everyday account, transfer it to your special untouchable account for future use.

For the readers who have an existing home loan, simply pretend that interest rates have just risen by 2% and raise your loan repayments accordingly. In a month or so, you will be used to the extra payments and you will have given yourself a safety buffer if rates rise. If they don't, you will save tens of thousands of dollars of interest.

If you don't have a home loan yet, and you are employed, ask the pay office to deduct at least 15% of your income before tax from your pay and have it credited to a bank account. You won't miss it and, as the weeks pass, you will be amazed at how quickly it grows.

The vault:

- Make investment a priority and do it in such a way that it happens automatically.

- You don't miss money you don't get.
- Money in your wallet gets blown on everyday items.
- Put the Guaranteed Secret of Wealth into practice.

23

HOW TO EARN MORE MONEY

Everything you want in life has a price connected to it. There's a price to pay if you want to make things better, a price to pay for leaving things as they are, a price for everything.

Harry Browne

In every country there is a massive gap between the income earned by the lowest and the highest paid people. In this chapter you'll learn why this is so and what is needed to put yourself in the higher income brackets.

Money is a medium that lets one person exchange goods and services for that of another. Therefore, it should be obvious that the more goods or services you can offer, the more money you are likely to receive in exchange. However, some goods and services are worth more than others. A shop assistant provides services, yet earns less for an hour's work than a teacher who may earn less than a plumber who, in turn, receives less than a doctor. Do you find this confusing? Not one of these individuals is any better than any other, and they all fill essential roles in our community. Why the difference in remuneration?

James says...

Steve Jobs, co-founder and CEO of Apple, was one of the innovators of modern information technology. In the 1970s and 1980s, he was instrumental in the development of personal computers and evolution of the IT industry. Now think about that in the context of the three points we discussed earlier – Jobs was in enormous demand, he was a leader in his field and would likely be very difficult to replace. Nonetheless, in 1985 the corporate structure of Apple squeezed him out and he was forced to pursue other interests.

Rather than dwell on his misfortune, Jobs saw this as a great opportunity and founded another IT company, which ended up being so valuable that it was purchased by Apple in 1996 for almost half a billion US dollars. History had proved that Jobs was irreplaceable and, in the mid-90s, he returned to Apple as CEO.

Here is the formula. The amount of money you are paid depends on:

(1)   The demand for your services.
(2)   How well you do what you do.
(3)   The difficulty in replacing you.

If you think about the above for a while, you may decide that being very good at what you do is the area on which to concentrate. That is the one over which you have most control. Also, if you are particularly good at what you do, the other two will fall into place naturally because your services will be in demand and you will certainly be hard to replace.

Now, you may think this pay system is a bit unfair. You might think the highest paid people should be school teachers or university lecturers because they have the responsibility of educating our next generation. You may feel doctors are most important because they can save lives and help bring babies into the world.

That might be fine in theory but in real life the system doesn't work like that. Your income is determined not by fairness but by the market. A popular author might write absolute garbage, but will be highly paid if enough people like to read what he or she turns out. Some television stars may receive a huge amount of money for making five 30-minute appearances every week. A sporting hero may earn a million dollars in one match. A rock group might receive more for a two-hour concert than most people earn for a year's work. That happens because there is a huge demand for their services and skills.

Noel says...

A client of mine owns a diamond and jewellery shop. When you walk into that shop, a woman, Mary, stands out. She has a bright look in her eye, is always happy and smiling, knows all the regular customers by name and is wonderful to deal with. Recently, I asked the owner how long she had been there. He replied, "Over 10 years and she is priceless. If she left I could not replace her." I have no doubt Mary receives a much higher salary than most other shop assistants in this country and that she would be swamped with offers if she ever decided to leave her present job.

Think about the other side of the coin, for it contains a valuable lesson for you. The **majority** of authors, television personalities, sports professionals and rock singers are in the lowest paid ranks of the workforce because so many people want to get into those "glamour" industries. They all want to make it big, but only a tiny number reach the top. Those that do are at the absolute peak of their profession. They are the best at what they do—at least in the public eye. The *Australian Idol* television series is immensely popular, and it revolves around the basic premise that only one person will win the competition and become famous. Have you ever wondered what happens to the tens of thousands who apply but don't win the competition? Apart from being forgotten very quickly by the viewers, they are usually destined to keep struggling with improving their craft to crack the big time. For many, this can be a very lonely existence.

All markets operate on the theory of supply and demand. The more people there are seeking the same kind of work, the less any one of them is likely to be paid. If you are a migrant with no specific skills and can hardly speak English, you may well end up doing process work in a factory where you are in danger of being replaced by a robot. Think about what would happen if you spent your entire working life with the one organisation in an administrative role and were then retrenched at the age of 50. It would be very difficult for you to find another job because there would probably be a whole group of retrenched people in a similar situation. Their job might also have been replaced by technology at a fraction of an expense to the employer.

It is often easier to find jobs if you are prepared to travel to remote areas because few people want to go there. A client of ours is now aged 65 and his services as a cost accountant are still in high demand because he will work in places like Indonesia or Dubai.

Remote jobs usually pay more than the equivalent position in the city and saving is easier in those places because there is often little to spend your money on. Many clients of our financial planning firm received their financial start in life by working in the country or in one of those non-glamorous overseas areas.

They set a goal to spend five years there, work long hours and build up a large sum of investment capital.

Now that you understand the relationship between employment markets and supply and demand, you will appreciate the importance of improving your skills. This will help you to become a member of the elite band whose skills are in demand, instead of being just another member of a large group chasing any job you can get. The top people in their fields always have job security as well as higher than average incomes.

YOU'VE GOT TO PUT IN THE HOURS

Those of you who want to earn your money in a more conventional way will find it will all fall into place if you practise what we have taught you in this book. Throughout the book we have stressed the importance of self-development and going the extra mile because this will enable you to develop the skills that will put you at the top of your chosen field. In the next chapter we will show you how to "multiply" yourself and move into the really high-earning field by progressing toward having your own business. However, when you are starting off, there is just no substitute for putting in the time.

The good news is that when you find the right path for yourself, the long hours don't matter because you will be enjoying what you do. Noel started writing this chapter at 4.45 on a Saturday morning in December, just a week before Christmas. He was holidaying at the beach and was sitting with his laptop on a patio overlooking the surf. The rest of the family was sleeping peacefully but he couldn't think of anything he would rather be doing.

What if you don't like working long hours? Find a hobby that you love doing or are passionate about—that way, you'll be on a lifelong holiday because you'll enjoy the time you spend on it. We have stressed that there is no connection between money and happiness, and you may have to settle for lower earnings if the field you enjoy does not return a huge income. If that is the case, go for what you enjoy.

Remember what we've discussed earlier—your rewards in life will match your service; therefore, the more time you put into developing your skills and providing service, the greater your rewards will be. Even if these rewards come in the form of personal satisfaction instead of money, you will have a fulfilled life.

HOW TO SCORE A PROMOTION

We will now let you inside an employer's mind and show you how to carve a fast track up the ladder of success. Let's pretend you are the owner of a small to medium-sized business, you have just lost one of your key staff and you have to find a replacement.

Like everybody else, you prefer a hassle-free existence—hiring and firing people isn't your thing. You know that hiring is always a problem because if you use a recruitment agency there are substantial fees to pay. But if you decide to find the person yourself there is the time-consuming process of creating the advertisements, screening all the applications, interviewing those who appear promising, making a final decision and then writing "sorry" letters to all those who missed out.

That can take weeks of your valuable time and, after it's all been done, there is no guarantee the person you choose will be suitable for the job. After a few months you might have to terminate their employment and start the whole time-consuming process all over again.

You know that firing a person is also difficult because few people are so bad that their behaviour warrants instant dismissal. Usually the performance is not quite as good as you hoped and, despite counselling and training, the feeling slowly but surely grows inside of you that this person is not suited for the job. Finally you decide they should go but your emotions get in the way (it may be their first job or they may be supporting a family) and you keep putting it off.

Eventually, after several months of internal strain, you take action or, if you are lucky, they leave and go elsewhere.

Of course, there is another way to approach the problem and it's one that progressive companies such as McDonald's generally use. That is, to select the replacement from the ranks of your existing staff members if possible.

As the proverb says, "The devil you know is better than the devil you don't", and you could save so much valuable time if you could look around your existing staff-base to see if one of them is suitable. Naturally, you would eliminate the stirrers, the latecomers, the procrastinators, those who spend half their time on personal phone calls and those who are more interested in themselves than your business. However, amongst your own people you will usually find that rare gem who does go the extra mile, who is keen to develop their skills and who is both competent and pleasant to work with. You might not give them the job immediately, but you will offer it to them on a temporary basis to see how they handle it. Usually they do it well and then you have made two people happy—yourself and the staff member who got the promotion.

In most companies there are people leaving regularly. This happens for many reasons that may include transfer of a spouse, a decision to start a family, failure to perform, travel, ill health or a better offer elsewhere. If you do what we have taught you in this book, you will be the one in the running for the promotion when the chance inevitably comes.

WHY EARN MORE MONEY?

We agree that it takes hard work and time to earn more money and many of you will be asking yourselves if the price is worth paying. Only you can answer that, but we urge you to give the question more than a passing thought before you give a negative answer. What do you honestly feel deep down? Do you lack the drive to do what needs to be done or are you frightened that you will do all the work and still not get the rewards? Do you doubt your own ability?

These are complex questions but a way to help find the right answer for you is to ask yourself what you would do if you won $10 million dollars today. If thoughts of a big home, exotic trips and expensive cars come to mind immediately, you do have a desire for material things. Any lack of motivation on your part is due to self-doubt or not knowing where to start. By the time you finish this book you will know where to start. Provided you make a start on your goals and your self-development program, there is no reason why you should not succeed.

Remember that earning more money will assist you to do the things you want to do and have the things you want to have. It will also help you in three important areas:

(1) It will provide a higher standard of living so you will have more money to spend each week.

(2)   You will have more money to invest, which means you will attain financial independence at an earlier age.

(3)   The skills you develop to earn the extra money will also assist you to reach your full potential, which we believe is your duty. Acquiring these skills will enable you to take advantage of many other valuable opportunities in the future.

The amount of money you earn is a reward for the service you give. The amount of money you have is a product of the techniques you use for retaining it and making it grow. Combine the skills of earning and investing, and financial independence is assured.

The vault:

- The more goods or services you can offer, the more money you are likely to receive.
- The amount you are paid depends on the demand for your services, how well you perform and the difficulty of replacing you.
- Markets operate on supply and demand—the more people there are seeking the same kind of work, the lower the pay is likely to be.
- When you are starting off, there is just no substitute for putting in the time.
- Make the right impression. Be the one who puts in the effort, arrives early, stays late, offers to help out where possible and constantly improves their skills.

- The amount of money you have is a product of the techniques you use for retaining it and making it grow. Combine the skills of earning and investing and financial independence is assured.

24

GO FOR PROFITS NOT WAGES

There is no security on this earth; there is only opportunity.

General Douglas MacArthur

If you've got this far you should be aware that we believe a happy and successful life means you are in control of it. Now we'll explain why one of the best ways to be in control is for you to have your own business.

Don't let your eyes glaze over and say, "Who, me? Own my own business!?" If you follow the principles in this book, you will be way ahead of "most people" and ultimately you will be able to achieve any realistic goals you set. Therefore, moving towards a position where you can start your own business should not be nearly as scary as it may sound.

But first, a word of warning—we promised you a happy and fulfilled life, not one that was hassle-free. If you run a business, you will still have plenty of hassles because you will be at the mercy of your customers, your staff, the bank manager, suppliers, economic cycles and every branch of government. But it's worth it.

Benefits of having your own business:

- You will have much more freedom
- You control your own income

- You can be flexible with your time and choose what hours you work
- You can choose when you want to have holidays
- You decide the ultimate direction of the company
- You are your own boss.

It is also one of the best ways to use the skills you have gained by personal development because you will succeed or fail on your merits.

If you are not too comfortable with the idea of succeeding or failing on your merits, you have missed the whole point of this book. Let me repeat it.

We believe that:

- All of us can choose success
- Success is predictable, and
- Success involves carrying out certain steps and it requires you to develop appropriate skills.

If that is not true, then it's all a matter of luck or being born to the right parents and, if **that's** true, we're all wasting our time trying to change what can't be changed!

Being in business means you are providing a service that people want. It may be:
- A security service to protect residential homes
- A store that sells cheap bait and fishing supplies
- An accounting service to help individuals or companies with tax and bookkeeping
- An online store that sells discounted sports memorabilia
- A financial planner to guide people with their investments
- A website development company offering low-cost solutions for small businesses
- A restaurant specialising in a certain type of cuisine
- A personal trainer to assist people with their fitness and health goals.

We could fill up this book with different services but if you stop for a few minutes to browse through the Yellow Pages (or their website) you will be amazed at the huge range of businesses there are. The only limits to new business ideas are the limits you place on your own imagination.

You have probably heard an expression that is used in financial planning circles, "The higher the risk, the higher the reward". It works for business, too, because going into business often involves taking risks. People in business usually work long hours and, when they are starting off, take on commitments such as big mortgages and long leases. They do this for the rewards of more income, the freedom of being their own boss and for the glorious feeling of being able to say, "This is my business and it will survive or perish because of my actions". They also face the possibility of losing everything they have if it goes bad.

LEARNING A LESSON

Noel says...

I learned that profits were better than wages in 1963 when I was a young impoverished bank officer earning around $40 a week.[34] I had struck up a friendship that endures to this day with a larger than life character named Eric. He left school at 14 and worked as a shop assistant for a while, but discovered that his lifestyle needed more than a shop assistant's wages and had promptly started selling real estate. My first memories of our friendship are of him spending each weekend sitting on a vacant estate waiting for buyers. You could see the ground through the rust holes in the floor of his car.

---

[34] This was before the introduction of decimal currency. The figures are converted to dollars for ease of understanding.

Eventually, his hard work began to pay off. By 1963, when he was 28, he owned a string of properties. One property was a commercial building that housed his own office, as well as one of Brisbane's most prominent illegal gambling dens. We had been having a few drinks when Eric decided he would buy some cheese to take home to his wife. He handed over four dollars and we walked off with a huge round block of cheese. On the way home he decided to broaden my knowledge by taking me for a tour of the premises of his main tenant—the gambling den.

We walked up the stairs, pressed the buzzer, gave the right password, and the huge solid steel door opened. I had expected an elegant atmosphere, but found myself in a smoky room that was crammed with tables occupied by foreign-looking men in grubby working clothes. There were huge piles of banknotes on each table. The proprietor of this establishment was Louie and he was bemoaning the fact that he needed some snacks to keep his clients' minds off their stomachs and on the gambling. Eric announced he had a large block of cheese that would do the job perfectly. "Fine," said Louie. "How much?" Quick as a flash Eric came back with, "Twenty dollars!!"

Louie happily pulled a $20 note from the huge roll he had in his pocket and we were on *our way. Eric had just made more in five minutes than I could make in two full days at the bank.*

THE POWER OF MULTIPLYING YOURSELF

When you have your own business you can multiply your efforts by employing others. As you know, most business people employ staff and when they work out what to charge their customers they calculate the cost of materials, if appropriate, and also add a margin for staff wages and other overheads. This means the boss must make a profit out of the staff to cover the other costs of the business and to provide a profit. This is where the leverage comes in.

Imagine you are a top gardener and can earn $25 an hour. The most you can ever earn is the number of hours you work multiplied by $25. Even if you worked to the point of exhaustion for, say, seven days a week for 10 hours a day, $1,750 a week is the limit of your income.

However, imagine how much more you could earn if you had a team of people working for you and you co-ordinated them to make the best use of their skills combined with yours. Maybe you are supervising the job, paying your gardeners $15 an hour, your labourers $12 an hour and juniors $8 an hour and yet are still charging out the whole job at $25 an hour. You could increase your income even further by selling products such as plants, fertilisers, sleepers and soil and making a profit on those as well. Now your income is limited only by the size of the operation you can manage and not by the hours of physical work you can do.

The founders of the giant Amway Corporation are Rich De Vos and Jay van Andel. They are both qualified pilots and started their business careers by giving flying lessons. Life changed for them when they worked out they could make far more money by selling flying lessons and hiring other pilots to give the lessons than to teach people to fly themselves. They had learned the power of multiplying themselves.

USING YOUR INITIATIVE

Let us take you back several years when we lived on a four-hectare property. Our young friend Ben lived nearby and he had been mowing our lawns and helping us in the garden for quite some time. He was only seven when his father died tragically but this had not stopped his drive. He earned his first few dollars by mowing lawns and by finding and selling lost golf balls at the nearby golf course. When the land around us was cut up for development Ben noticed there were up to 60 workers on site at any one time. He started buying cases of soft drinks at wholesale prices, chilling them and selling them to the workers for a profit of 50 cents a can. He did this by pushing a huge wheelbarrow with an icebox full of drinks around the sites. As his sales increased, he expanded his range to include chocolate bars and sandwiches (which he paid his mother to make for him).

Ben is far more than just a delightful young man; he always goes the extra mile. Because we had quite a large property with a huge expanse of lawns and gardens, Ben continually found new areas that needed a mow or a clip.

Although we haven't spoken to Ben in a while, we have no doubt he will be a success at whatever he decides to do.

We suggest you establish a little business of your own as soon as possible in order to gain an idea and understanding of what it takes. The skills needed to run a business include marketing, pricing, arranging supplies, doing what you promise and putting up with the whims of customers. If you like the idea of selling you could consider a multilevel marketing (a form of network marketing) operation such as Amway, Nutrimetics or Tupperware to name just a few[35]. Here you will gain invaluable experience and personal growth as well as making some useful pocket money.

If you don't find that appealing, you could try some casual work in a small business. This may be at the local store, at the bottle shop, night-fill at a large supermarket or even delivering brochures. The type of work is not important be-

---

[35] The names are listed in alphabetical order. There are many such reputable companies to consider.

cause at this stage the purpose of doing it is to give you an insight into the way a business functions.

After a few years working for somebody else, you could now think about a career and establishing your own business. You will also find many obvious fits, such as:
- A police officer can start a security business
- A union official can become an industrial relations consultant
- A carpenter can become a builder
- A gym assistant can start a personal training business
- A hotel employee may start a small restaurant.

Once you become experienced in your field, you will find that opportunities present themselves.

As this chapter comes to an end, think again about the words of General MacArthur that started it off. There is no security, only opportunity. This century will bring the most extraordinary opportunities for those who are prepared for them. If you can run your own business effectively in this climate, the rewards will be there for the taking.

The vault:

- Owning your own business is a very challenging, yet rewarding, experience that allows you to be more in control of your life.
- Being in business means you are providing a service that people want.

- The only limits to new business ideas are the limits you place on your own imagination.
- When you have your own business you can multiply your efforts by employing others.

25

INVESTING THE FIRST MONEY YOU MAKE

Money is not the only answer but it makes a difference.

Barack Obama

Every week we receive emails from young people along the lines of "I have saved $5,000—where should I invest it?" It is not a question that can be answered in a couple of words because before you decide where to invest the money, you must decide what you are trying to achieve.

For example, if you are saving for a car or a house you should stick with the online accounts offered by the major lending organisations. There are no entry or exit fees, your money is available on demand, and you have no risk of loss if the stock market has one of its inevitable falls.

But, if you want that money to be the foundation of a long term investment portfolio and are prepared to leave it untouched for at least 10 years, you should consider property or shares.

There may appear to be a dazzling array of invest-ment opportunities around but almost every investment falls into one of two categories—debt investments or equity investments.

When you make a debt investment you deposit money with an establishment such as a bank, building society or credit union which in turn lend it out to people who wish to borrow it. Your return is solely from the interest you receive.

When you make an equity investment you invest it in areas such as real estate, shares, gold or antiques. It changes character and in some cases you may receive income (rent for property, dividends from shares) and also some capital gain.

Which category is right for you? That depends on what you are trying to achieve. There is no perfect investment that will be all things to all people so don't waste your time looking for it. Instead take the time to understand the good and bad points of each type of investment so you will be able to choose the ones that are best for you.

Debt Investments

The most common form of debt investment is a bank account. When you put $2,000 in the bank you can be fairly certain that when you come to withdraw it the $2,000 will still be there, plus whatever interest it may have earned in the meantime. As a rule, there are no charges when you deposit or withdraw, but there may be bank fees for keeping the account.

Advantages:

- Certainty of the money being there when you need it.
- The lack of costs for depositing and withdrawing.
- The ability to withdraw all or part of it at short notice.

Disadvantages:

- You are liable to pay tax on the interest, and the rate of this tax may rise as your other income rises.
- Lack of capital growth. Money is only worth what it can buy, and each year this is reduced by inflation. If you left that $2,000 in the bank for five years you may then find that it would buy far less than it would buy now. This is called inflation. If you want to see it in practice, speak to your parents or grandparents about the price of goods and

services when they were young compared to the prices today.

Equity Investments

There are many equity investments but the most common are real estate and shares.

Advantages:

- The opportunity to receive a higher return overall than you would if you left your money in the bank (due to income and capital gain).
- Capital gains tax (the tax on the capital gain) is taxed at a lower rate than income tax. It is not due until the investment is sold and even then is reduced by 50% if you have the asset for more than a year.

Disadvantages:

- Fees to invest and withdraw.
- Your money may drop in value.

Let's imagine you had saved up $5,000 for a trip you wanted to take next year. You decided to invest it in shares because you heard there was a boom about to happen and there were bundles of money to be made. If you invested the $5,000 in shares you would have to pay the stockbroker up to $150 (3%) when you bought them (online trading accounts such as Commsec offer brokerage from as low as $30 if you know what you want to buy), which has reduced your original capital by 3% immediately. There is a further 3% to pay when you sell, but the dollar amount of this will depend on the selling price. If you struck it lucky and your shares rose to $6,000 (a 20% gain) the selling brokerage would be $180. Thus, your total buying and selling costs are $330 or 6.6% of the initial value.

If the shares had stayed around their original value, you would still have been liable for brokerage of $150 when you sold them. That's equal to 6% of your original capital. Unless the shares gain in value by 6% you have not broken even and would have done much better by leaving your money in the bank.

The other problem with equity investments is highlighted by the rule "Wherever there is a chance of a capital gain there is a chance of a capital loss". What if the market slumped suddenly (as happened in the 1987 crash or during the 2007–2009 global financial crisis) and the value of your shares dropped by 40% or more? You could find that your $5,000 had dwindled to less than $3,000.

Real estate and share investments should be the foundation of any long-term investment portfolio and we are not highlighting their disadvantages to put you off placing money in these areas. Nevertheless, it is important you understand they should only be used in the right circumstances and that placing money in these areas is a long-term project.

Most young people have the savings goals of a car, a house and travel. In many cases, the money for these is best placed in the interest-bearing area. However, depending on the timeframe, a regular savings plan through a balanced unit trust might be appropriate.

A balanced unit trust is a pool of money, managed by a fund manager, that is invested in both debt and equity investments. The fund would normally have its money invested in interest-bearing accounts, government bonds, local and overseas shares and real estate. Investments in these type of products are usually made through licensed financial advisers.

ALL EARNINGS ARE NOT EQUAL

When deciding where to invest, keep in mind that all earnings are not equal. The money you receive in your pay packet would normally come from your own efforts and this is taxed at normal personal tax rates. If you are a low-income earner, your tax may be as low as 15%, but if you are a high-income earner it could be as high as 45%.

You can also receive earnings by way of capital gain, as happens if you buy property and shares and they rise in value. The great thing about capital gain is that it is not taxed until you dispose of the asset, which may be many years away if you follow our advice of holding for the long term. Furthermore, if you hold the asset for more than a year, you receive a 50% discount on the tax payable of that capital gain. As a result, even the highest income earners pay no more than 23.25% capital gains tax on the sale of assets that they have held for over a year.

Franked dividends (which carry imputation credits) also offer great tax concessions. Before the Hawke/Keating government introduced imputation in July 1987, shareholders suffered double taxation on their dividends. First, the companies paid tax on any profits they made. Then the shareholders were taxed again when they received these tax-paid profits as dividends. As the top marginal tax rates then were over 60% it meant the total tax-take could be as high as 78%.

Since then, dividends from companies that have borne the Australian company tax rate carry imputation credits. The word "impute" means to "give credit for" and this is exactly what the imputation system does. It allows shareholders to receive credit for the tax paid by any company in which they hold shares, and pay tax only on the difference between that and their own tax rate.

If you owned 10,000 shares in a company and it paid a franked dividend of seven cents a share, your dividend would be $700 and would carry with it imputation credits of $300 as a result of the tax already paid by the company.

You are entitled to use those credits to pay your own tax—in other words they are as good as cash, but only if you spend the money at the Tax Office. As the credits represent value, you have to pay tax on them. Yes, even though you received only $700, you have to declare $1,000 ($700+$300) as taxable income. That's the bad part. Now comes the good bit. You can use those credits to offset your tax bill and possibly even reduce it.

Let's look at how that works in practice.

Jack's earnings	$70,000
Less income tax	15,000
Income after tax	$55,000
Jack's earnings	$70,000
Shares (dividend plus franking credit)	10,000
	$80,000
Less income tax	18,000
Income after tax	$62,000

Jack earns $70,000 a year on which tax is $15,000 a year. He buys a portfolio of shares that produce franked dividends of $7,000 a year as well as providing $3,000 of imputation credits. When he does his tax return he will have to add $10,000 to his taxable income—that's the sum of the dividend plus the franking credit—which will take his taxable income to $80,000. His tax bill will rise by $3,000 to $18,000 because of the extra $10,000 of income. However, he now has the use of those $3,000 worth of imputation credits. They wipe out that tax on the dividend so it becomes tax-free and he only has to pay tax on his regular earnings.

If Jack had earned that extra $7,000 from bank interest, he would have had to pay $2,100 tax on it and would have no opportunity for capital gain. This is what makes shares paying franked dividends so popular with experienced investors, and why shares are such a great investment for those people who can handle volatility.

It's even better for lower income investors, as they can claim a refund of unused franking credits. If you earned $24,000 a year and received $7,000 in franked dividends, the tax on those dividends would be just $1,500 but you would be entitled to $3,000 in franking credits. For you, the dividends wouldn't just be tax-free—they would carry a bonus of $1,500 as well. This means an 8% franked dividend is providing them with an after tax return of 9.71%.

Now let's look at the powerful combination of capital gains and franked dividends. Suppose Mary is very successful and earns $250,000 from her job. Tax would take almost $90,000, leaving her with $160,000.

Mary's friend Brenda no longer has to work because she has built a large portfolio of shares over the years, which is now worth $5 million and returns $500,000 a year comprised of 5% growth and 5% franked dividends. There is no tax on the $250,000 of growth because she doesn't sell any shares in the year and, because the income is franked, it includes $107,000 of franking credits.

Yes, Brenda will have to add the franking credits to her taxable income so will be paying tax on $357,000. Accordingly, her tax will be $138,000. Fortunately, she has $107,000 to offset against her $138,000 tax liability so will only face a tax bill of $31,000.

The numbers might look complicated but, put simply, both women received income of $250,000. Mary paid tax of $90,000 whereas Brenda paid tax of just $31,000.

This is why it is so important to start building your portfolio at an early age. Far too many young, high-income earners think earning the big money is all that matters—they confuse that earning with building assets and, accordingly, get to age 30 with very little to show for 10 years of work.

RENT OR BUY?

We appreciate that buying a home and paying it off is a worthy goal and has been the foundation of wealth for most of us. However, in most locations it's always cheaper to rent than to buy and there is really no reason to rush into the property market unless you see prices start to surge.

For example, think about a property that costs $350,000 and can be rented for $400 a week. If you rent it, the total cost is $20,800 a year. If you buy it, you will be up for at least $27,000 a year when you take interest rates and maintenance into account. That's over $6,000 a year in favour of the renter. And there are often many other costs when you own your home. There is nothing truer than the Scottish proverb "A wee house has a wide mouth" because there's always something popping up that needs repair or replacement.

As the example above shows, a couple who rented for two years would have an extra $12,000 to use as a deposit when they eventually did buy. This would create savings in two areas—it would eliminate the need for costly mortgage insurance, as well as saving a large amount of interest.

Let's look at that in detail. You are keen to buy a house for $350,000 and now have a deposit of $35,000 plus legal fees after the first homeowner's grant is taken into account. If you buy now, you will need to borrow $315,000 but this could rise to $320,000 when the once-only mortgage insurance premium is added. Repayments over 25 years would be $2,262[36] a month and the total interest payable $363,600—you would be paying $678,600 for the property.

If you rent for two more years, and save diligently, you may be able to get by with a loan of $290,000. There would be no mortgage insurance, as you are not borrowing more than 80% of the purchase price. Repayments of $2,262 a month on the $290,000 loan would enable you to pay the loan off in just under 20 years with interest payments of $252,880. Taking the

---

[36] The interest rate used in the examples on this page is 7%. This rate may not reflect what is currently available.

time to save for a bigger deposit has enabled you to save over $100,000.

As you can see, there is a strong prima facie case for renting, provided property values don't jump while you're busily saving your deposit. However, if a boom ever gets under way again, you'd better buy in a hurry, lest you be caught in the situation where house prices are rising quicker than you can save. No, we don't have a crystal ball, and we don't know which way property prices in your area are going to move. However, we can tell you that savvy property buyers spend every waking hour researching the property market in their area so they know where the trend is heading and will recognise a bargain when they finally come across one. This does take time (and a lot of work) and it includes befriending local agents, keeping track of sales in the area, going to open houses and generally knowing everything about the local property market.

If you become one of these savvy buyers, you'll develop a knowledge of property in your local area over time and you will eventually know more about the market than the majority of buyers and sellers. The reward will be that one day you will strike a situation where a desperate vendor has a property for sale in a great location. You will be the one who will be able to steal the bargain.

INVEST OR BUY A HOUSE?

Young people often wonder whether they should focus all their energies on saving for a house deposit with the ultimate aim of having their own home, or whether they should invest elsewhere. There is no easy answer because the best strategy depends on your own personal circumstances. For example, if you are only 18 and can't see yourself buying a house for 10 years, you are probably better to build a good share-based investment portfolio. As we explained previously, you will then receive tax concessions in the way of income from franked dividends that will almost certainly be tax-free for you, capital gains will be only lightly taxed and you will not be liable for that until you sell the shares to raise the deposit for your house.

The benefit of doing this is the experience you will get in watching the share market rise and fall. You'll also practise the strategy of dollar cost averaging (investing a set sum in the same investment every month) because you can buy shares in small parcels.

A further advantage is that over 10 years shares can provide much better returns than leaving your money in the bank where it will be attacked by inflation and you will be paying full tax on the interest.

Of course, the major disadvantage is that share prices can plunge (as in 1987 and 2008). A way to reduce the negative effects of this is to watch the balance closely as you get to within two or three years of buying your home. If you have had very good capital gains and you see the market fall by 15%, it may be time to cash out then to avoid further capital losses. This is a very rough rule of thumb and you should always take into account prevailing circumstances.

A common question from people who invest in shares while they are waiting to buy a house is whether they should keep the shares and borrow the maximum amount for the house. This is not a good strategy because over the long term you should be seeking to maximise your deductible debt and minimise your non-deductible debt. Usually you are better off to cash in the shares, pay whatever capital gains tax is necessary, and then have the biggest deposit possible. Once you are well established in your home, you can always take out a home equity loan to buy back into the share market. The interest on this loan will be highly tax deductible and, as the loan is secured by a mortgage over the home, you are most unlikely to get a margin call.

It is a different matter if you are older and intend to buy a house within two to three years. In this situation you cannot afford to lose any of your capital in entry or exit fees, and you certainly don't want to put yourself in a position where you will lose money if the market falls. You are much better off to stick with the online interest-bearing accounts offered by the major banks until you are ready to buy the house.

BUYING PROPERTY WITH FRIENDS

Many would-be investors are wary of shares and, as a result, only feel comfortable with direct ownership of real estate that may well be out of their reach. Therefore, it frequently happens that those with some spare money to invest consider pooling it with friends, or with members of their family, and going into a real estate joint venture.

Going into a joint investment does not happen only when the parties feel their individual resources are too small to allow them to act individually. Often these ventures start because members of the family think it would be fun, as well as profitable, to undertake a project together, or because one of them acquires some money as a result of a windfall gain, such as a legacy or lottery win.

In our experience, such activities are fraught with danger and the outcome is often the end of the friendship between the parties as well as the loss of a large sum of money. When things start to go wrong, they often go horribly wrong, and the original good intentions, trust and tolerance are quickly forgotten. *Time* magazine quoted the American policeman George Napper who let forth with the now famous lines "When you're up to your ass in alligators, it's hard to remember that your purpose is draining the swamp!"

One of the major difficulties can be caused by differences in the temperaments of the parties involved. Some investors are aggressive, some are timid, some like to make decisions quickly and others like to mull over them for days. Put two different investment personalities together and you have a recipe for strife. Consider the following example.

Emily and Sophie were single sophisticated women in their late 20s. They decided to cash in on the property boom by buying an investment unit for $300,000, putting in $15,000 each and borrowing the balance. The first problem arose when they came to finance it. Emily was an aggressive investor who wished to borrow on an interest only basis using a five-year fixed interest mortgage—the method used by most serious investors.

Sophie was a less adventurous borrower who felt people who borrowed on an interest-only basis never got anywhere because the debt did not reduce. She plugged for a short-term principal and interest loan. Emily stood firm and Sophie reluctantly went along with the interest-only loan.

Then came the decision of who was going to manage it. Sophie wanted a real estate agent to do it, because she felt nervous dealing with tenants; Emily believed this was a total waste of 10% of the rent and persuaded Sophie to agree.

Emily was an ambitious person and found her workload was increasing. She began leaving more of the rental management and maintenance to Sophie who started to resent doing the lion's share of the work. Friction started to build and the situation worsened when Emily was transferred to an executive position in another city, leaving her friend with the job of all the management.

By this stage, Sophie had met her dream partner and had far better things to occupy her spare time than being involved with property management. She and her fiancée decided to buy a house to live in but, to find her share of the deposit, Sophie had to sell the investment house. Only then did she realise there would be a large penalty for paying out the loan before the end of the agreed term. Emily was not happy either. She was liable for a large sum in capital gains tax because of her large salary. It was the end of a good friendship.

A similar problem would arise if one of the women lost their job and could not make up the required monthly contributions. The one who is unemployed is likely to insist the house be placed on the market so that she can fulfil her obligations, but this may coincide with a time when the market is in one of it long, flat spells.

Unfortunately, real estate is an investment that usually needs time to produce a large profit. A forced sale, too soon after purchase, could result in a loss. People's situations never stay static. The high-income earner of today may be unemployed tomorrow. The single person with no thought of marriage may be walking down the aisle within a year.

Joint ownership also costs investors flexibility. Here's a typical situation.

Josh and Mia work for the same company and buy a property in joint names as an investment. They plough all their spare cash into paying it off and are almost debt-free when Josh unexpectedly receives an opportunity to go into a promising business venture. He wants to mortgage his share of the property to borrow the funds for the capital he needs but there are immediate problems.

Mia regards his venture as risky and will not consent to a mortgage over the property. As a result, Josh cannot raise finance because he cannot find a lender who would accept a second mortgage over half a property. It's a case of miss out on the venture or sell the property.

REGULAR GEARING

Noel says...

It's great to see young people preparing for their future but it can be a challenge when you see them heading down one path when experience tells you they would probably be better off taking a different one.

These thoughts came to mind when I was having a coffee with a friend whose son has made it big in the sports world and is looking forward to at least 10 years of high income. I've known the young man since he was in kindergarten and he is fortunate to have come from a family with a strong work ethic and a habit of saving. My friend said, "He is really doing well and we are thrilled that he understands that the next few years may be the turning point in his life. He has resolved not to waste his money on things like flash cars but is determined to put a financial foundation in place that will set him up for the rest of his life."

Of course, this was a good reason for congratulations but it also begged the question of what strategies the son was going to do to get himself on the road to financial independence. The reply was, "He's buying units off the plan."

Ouch! Warning bells rang immediately because it has been my experience that profits in real estate come from the land content, not the building content, which makes well-located houses much better long-term investments than units. I said, "Surely he'd be better off getting into shares as they have much greater potential than units off the plan." He replied, "I mentioned shares to him but he doesn't know a thing about shares and, in any event, can't afford to take a risk—he feels much more comfortable with bricks and mortar."

So what do you do? There was no way I was going to say anything negative to dampen the young bloke's enthusiasm but I also felt a strong responsibility to encourage him to look at shares as well. Good shares are not high risk if kept for the long term. In fact, staying away from shares is a much riskier proposition than investing in them.

The solution that came to mind was an each-way bet. By all means invest in property if that's where he feels safe, but the great advantage of shares over property is that you can start with as little as $1,000—you don't have to get into hock for hundreds of thousands of dollars as you do with property.

My advice was to start a regular gearing plan. He could start with $1,000 and then invest $300 a month into a quality Australian share trust—this would be matched with up to $600 of borrowed money. His total investment would be $900 a month and after a year he would have invested a total of $10,800, of which $3,600 was from his own funds and $7,200 was borrowed. For a person like my friend's son it was the perfect investment because it would allow him to experience the benefit of share ownership gradually and at the same time enjoy the benefits of dollar cost averaging. If the market fell in the next few months, the same monthly investment would buy more units in the trust.

As a further benefit this strategy would enable him to compare the returns from both property and shares over a five-year period *and also gain invaluable knowledge of the different ways these two asset classes perform.*

Now I guess you're thinking that a piddling $900 a month wouldn't amount to much. However, if he had started in January 1990 and invested the money in a managed fund that matched the All Ordinaries Accumulation Index, the portfolio would have been worth $604,433 as at 31 August 2009. He would have invested a total of $70,800 of his own money and the debt would now be $141,600. The total outlay to control over $600,000 worth of shares is just $300 a month plus the tax-deductible interest on the growing loan. It will be interesting to see if buying units off the plan can beat that.

SUPERANNUATION

Unfortunately, there is a general feeling in the community that superannuation is an extremely complex topic and is better off avoided. Nothing could be further from the truth. You need to understand that superannuation is not an asset like property or shares but merely a vehicle that lets you hold assets in a low tax area. Because the government does not want you holding a vast amount of money in a low tax area, they have restricted the amount that can be contributed by putting a cap on contributions. Also, you lose access to the money you have in super until you reach your preservation age which, for people born after June 1964, is aged 60. This makes superannuation unsuitable as a savings vehicle for young people but it still enables you to save some tax.

Suppose you are earning $65,000 a year and, after doing your budget and reviewing your debts, decide that you will need $300,000 of life and total and permanent disability (TPD) insurance on which the yearly premium is $380. This type of insurance is not tax deductible so you have to pay it from after tax dollars. Therefore, the cost to your pay packet would be $555 because this is the amount you would have to earn less 31.5% tax to have $380.

However, if you salary sacrificed $380 from your salary into super and then paid the insurance premium out of the super fund, the entire pre-tax cost of the insurance would be $380—that's a saving of $175 or $3.36 a week. Now that mightn't sound much but this type of strategy will get you into the habit of thinking about saving tax and will pay you dividends over the long term.

You may also find that your super fund itself offers life and TPD insurance at cheaper rates than you can buy it yourself because they can bulk buy on behalf of all their members (your financial adviser will be able to help you with this).

Even though superannuation is not an ideal investment vehicle for a very young person because their money is tied up to age 60 at least, in the right circumstances it can be a very useful tool to turn a small amount into a large sum. It can also provide invaluable financial education during the investor's working life.

Think about a 17-year-old who has a part-time job. Provided they earn less than $31,920 a year, they will be eligible for the full government superannuation co-contribution. All they (or their parents) have to do is find $1,000 a year (less than $20 a week) for an undeducted contribution to super and the government will give them a cocontribution of $1,000. It's money for nothing and after just three years they will have a superannuation balance of almost $7,000 made up of $3,000 of their own contributions and $3000 from the government.

Of course, the employer will be paying super for them too but for the purposes of this example we are ignoring it (the employer 9% contribution is not enough in these days of rising life expectancies). The aim of this example is to show how the magic of compounding can magnify additional contributions.

If we assume the superannuation fund earns 10% and they keep up the extra contributions until age 24, their superannuation balance then will be around $24,000. At this stage, they may decide they have other priorities such as buying a home, or their income may be at a level where they are no longer eligible for a large co-contribution. However, if no more personal contributions were made, and the fund continued to earn 10%, the balance of their fund would be $1,423,000[37] at age 65. It's a magnificent outcome—remember this is **in addition** to the employer superannuation. And all for a total investment of just $8,000 of their own money plus the government co-contribution!

There are other benefits. By the time our hypothetical worker is 24, they will have established the savings habit, they will have at least $24,000 of capital that they can control (but cannot withdraw), and will then have at least 40 years to learn how to invest that money via their superannuation fund to achieve the maximum return and, in the process, become experienced in the normal ups and downs of world stock markets. Most super funds allow the member to go online, check on their investment options – for example, Australian shares, growth funds, international shares, the money market etc.—and then make their investment choices. A person who has been investing in shares for a long period is not going to turn a paper loss into a real one by cashing in a quality portfolio when the market has one of its inevitable slumps.

You could put an argument that the money they invested in super between age 17 and 24 could be better used to fund the purchase of a car or to boost their deposit for a home. True, but we are not talking about large sums of money here. Irrespective of age or income, it's human nature to pay our commitments

---

[37] These figures were calculated using the Noel Whittaker Wealth Creator on CD-ROM.

and then spend the balance. If the paltry sum of $20 a week was taken from their account by direct debit, it wouldn't be missed and they would be setting themselves up to have an additional million dollars when they retire. Today, many young people think nothing of running up $100 a month on their mobile phone or spending $10 for a cocktail!

The vault:

- Before you decide where to invest, decide what you are trying to achieve.
- There may appear to be a dazzling array of investment opportunities around but almost all are either debt investments or equity investments.
- Take the time to understand the good and bad points of each investment type so you can make the best personal choice.
- Real estate and share investments should be the foundation of any long-term portfolio.
- Savvy property buyers thoroughly research the property market in their area so they know where the trend is heading and can recognise a bargain.
- Good shares are not high risk if kept for the long term.
- People's situations never stay static.
- Superannuation is not an asset like property or shares but merely a vehicle that lets you hold assets in a low tax area.

26

GETTING GOING

A mind stretched to a new idea never goes back to its original dimensions.

Oliver Wendell Holmes

When Noel put down *Think and Grow Rich* he knew his life could never be the same again. It was as if a veil had been lifted from his eyes and he could suddenly see clearly for the first time. Our wish is that you will be now feeling this way too. If you can start to look at yourself and your life in a fresh way, you are well on the road to success.

Treat this book as a key that has opened the gate to a new path. For a while you will be like a foal on wobbly legs as you take those first hesitant steps along the way. You will fall over, you will face set-backs, and often things won't happen as you planned. However, you will slowly make progress as the habits of success take over your thinking. Like compound interest, that progress will gather speed as time passes.

There is no doubt the future will present extraordinary opportunities to those who are prepared. Technology will continue to boom, requiring highly skilled people to maintain the machines and write the software. Travel and its associated industries (such as accommodation and restaurants) will be crying out for good staff while the most competent people in the building trades area will be sought after. There will continue to be breakthroughs in science and medicine, and many openings will appear for work with the ageing. As ever, top marketing and sales people will be prized. There will be a strong demand for financial advisers, accountants and lawyers as regulations and laws become more complex. There will not be enough good people around to fill the vacancies.

Let's cast our minds back on what you have read to date. We started by saying we were concerned by the lack of confidence being felt by young people but pointed out that you face a unique set of challenges that also provide great opportunities for those who know how to handle them. The aim of the book is to release the potential you have inside you so as to enable you to handle these new challenges.

In the first three chapters we described the potential in all of us and tried to help you define what success is for you. Certainly success means different things to different people and you must find your own path.

We moved into the problem areas in the next chapter when we introduced the concept of "most people". They are the majority who go through life wishing and hoping things will change but never do anything positive about it except buy Lotto tickets. If you choose to be "most people" you will waste your life dreaming instead of achieving.

In chapter five we showed you the magic formula that can start a chain reaction. It starts with a belief, which will begin moving to reality when you write down the goal. However, a goal without a plan to carry it through is nothing more than a wish. Only by making plans and taking action can you get what you want.

In chapters six and seven we introduced you to the idea of reframing and to the notion of self-concept. Undoubtedly, how we see ourselves has a huge effect on our performance but we live in a generally negative world where our brains are bombarded from birth with negative images. The way to improve your self-concept is to slowly form the habit of achieving little successes so that each small success gives you the confidence to try the next one. Eventually you will start to think of yourself as a person who can solve your own problems, instead of being a victim in a world over which you have no control.

The law of sowing and reaping, covered in chapter eight, is such an obvious one that you would wonder why it needs to be mentioned at all. Yet "most people" spend their lives trying to reap the crop without planting the seed. Consequently, as Henry David Thoreau said, "The mass of men lead lives of quiet desperation."[38]

In chapters nine and 10 we discussed the importance of goal setting and gave you three essential skills to speed your journey on the road to success. These are getting into the habit of going the extra mile, gaining some basic sales skills and learning to speak in public. A person who can do these three things has jumped into the top 5% of the population because so few will even attempt them.

Chapter 11 repeats the theme of the book—in order to have more, you must become more. We should think of life as a continual "do it yourself" process.

Chapter 12 contains the vital but perhaps sad message that we must fail in order to succeed because the only way to increase our value is to learn new skills. Every new skill takes pain and effort—hence the expression "No gain without pain". We followed this by stressing the importance of having a positive mental attitude. It is well documented that those who

---

38   Thoreau, Henry David. (1817–1862) Walden.

think in positive terms achieve positive results, and that a positive mental attitude is an essential attribute of a winner.

We continued in this vein in chapter 14 by urging you to try as many new experiences as possible so as to speed up your personal development. Next came the universal laws (chapter 15), which may have appeared strange to you at first, as they are concerned with opposites. To receive, you first have to give, and often your best successes come out of your failures. In the following chapter we faced the reality that your life is in your hands, no one else's.

By this stage, you were two thirds through the book and the lessons turned to finance because money plays such a large part in our society. There is no doubt that nothing can take the place of money in the areas where money works.

These include giving you access to a better education, a higher standard of living and the ability to make more choices in your life.

Knowing about interest is essential because the proper use of interest will allow you to speed up your own wealth creation, while an over reliance on borrowings has put many people in bankruptcy. We let you into the secret of compound interest and showed you why it is important to manage your money so as to build a capital base. The best way to do this is to use a budget, which ensures that every dollar is put to its best use. In chapter 23 we urged you to consider steps that would lead to you having your own business as this is the best way to increase your income. The book finished by discussing the range of investments that are suitable for the person who is starting off.

As we finish, understand that your brain is like your body—it needs regular food and exercise to function effectively. If this book is to be of lasting value you will have to regard it as the starting point on your road to success and continue to learn more about the subject. The Success Library that follows will help you.

Now may be an appropriate time to take a break and reflect on a little poem a friend of ours showed us as she was reading the manuscript. Unfortunately its origins are unknown.

There is an older person up there ahead of you, that you ought to know

That person looks like you, talks like you, walks like you

That person has your eyes, your nose, your chin and whether he or she hates you or loves you, respects you or despises you or is hungry or comfortable depends on you. You made that person.

That is you: ten years, twenty years, thirty years from now.

This is the final chapter in this book but we hope it will be the start of a new life for you. We can do no more than wish you good health and happiness on your road to wealth.

BUILDING A SUCCESS LIBRARY

BY

NOEL WHITTAKER

You are the same today as you will be in five years except for two things—the people you meet and the books you read.

Charles E. Jones.

Whenever I write, I think about a person I once met when I was doing a "book signing". Book signing involves sitting at a table in a busy street outside a book store autographing copies of your books for those who wish to buy them. To help attract a crowd, the store may hire a publicity person who, with the aid of a microphone and a large loud speaker, tries to entice people to stop and browse through the stacks of your books that cover the table. Occasionally a large group may gather around but more often almost everybody scurries by without giving you a second look.

The book signing I particularly remember took place at noon in Brisbane when I was signing copies of *Making Money Made Simple.* A young man walking by stopped to look at the book. He carried a pie and a can of Coke and he had a packet of cigarettes stuffed into a pocket on his sleeve. Obviously he worked on a nearby building site and there was an openness about him that appealed to me immediately.

He looked me up and down, put down the Coke, and picked up one of my books. Then he said with a smile "Do you reckon I could read this?". "Yes, I reckon you could read it" I replied. We had a bit of a chat about earning and spending money and then he carried the book to the counter to pay for it. As he left he said "You know, I've never read a book."

Can you imagine how I felt? Jim Rohn had taught me "We are all affected by the books we haven't read" and I am a fervent believer in the power of books to change lives.

I thought "What a responsibility I have. If he reads that book it may well change his life. Even if it doesn't, it might encourage him to read other books that may be of great help to him. If he finds my book boring, or heavy going, he probably won't finish it. Worse still, he may never pick up another book again."

Now you know why I write the way I do. Whenever I am reviewing what I have written I see that young man in my mind and think "Will he understand this?"

Just as a car needs petrol, so does your mind need continual doses of motivation and knowledge. This book will show you where the road starts but it will be of little lasting benefit to you unless you keep widening your knowledge.

THE POWER OF BOOKS

You have probably had older people say to you "I wish I was your age and knew what I know now". Well, you won't need to say that when you're their age because you have access to much of the knowledge that older people have taken a lifetime to accumulate. Through books and other material such as video, audiobooks and podcasts you can be young and know what they know now.

You can tap into some of the greatest minds that ever lived merely by going to a library or a book store, or spending a few minutes searching for articles on the internet. At one stage Og Mandino, who is now a famous writer, had bought a $30 revolver and was about to kill himself. However something inside him made him pause and search for answers instead. He writes:

I was just about as complete a failure as one can become. I began to spend a good deal of time in libraries looking for some answers. Where had I gone wrong? Was it too late for me? I found all the answers I needed in that golden vein of ore that every library has, that special shelf of books devoted to success, how to achieve it and how to hold on to it after one attains it. My counsellors were some of the wisest people who ever lived ... people like Elbert Hubbard, Norman Vincent Peale, W. Clement Stone, Napoleon Hill, Dale Carnegie, Maxwell Maltz, Louis

Binstock and Dorethea Brande. The advice from their books helped to change my life.

***

In this section we will show you how to start a success library by recommending eight books to start you off. Once you have finished these, you may be ready to search around and find other books you enjoy that will help you on your path to success. Once you get into the habit of reading books and listening to audio recordings, you will quickly discover what works for you and what doesn't.

In compiling the basic list we were conscious of the feedback from the young guy at the building site and have picked books that are easy to read and packed with useful information. Don't buy them all at once. Go to a good bookstore, browse through them and buy the one that feels right for you at the time. When you have read that one, buy another. When you have read all eight books you will probably be ready for a break and should look out for some good autobiographies.

HOW TO READ

Earlier in this book we mentioned the Buddhist saying "When the pupil is ready the teacher will appear". Just reading this book has taken you to a new level of awareness and you will find if you read it again you will understand it better because a different you is the reader. This "new you" will look at life in a different light and see things you hadn't seen before. The higher awareness you have achieved will enable you to understand more of life in general. And your awareness will grow still further as you continue the learning process.

Find a book store or library in which you feel comfortable and get to know the staff there. They will be able to guide you into areas of special interest and suggest books and authors who may appeal to you. If you have trouble finding a good book store, ask the most successful person you know where they get their books from.

Understand the awareness growing process and appreciate that a book that doesn't seem right today may well contain the answers you need in the future. When you start to put together your own library you will be amazed what will happen as you progress through life. You will be able to go to your library, select a book at random and find it contains just the answer to your problem.

When you are choosing books, watch the best seller lists in the newspapers and also look inside the front cover of a book to find the number of times it has been reprinted. If a book has been selling continually for years it is obvious that people are buying it and recommending it to their friends.

THE RICHEST MAN IN BABYLON by George Clason. Approximate price $20. The classic book on money that has been on the best seller lists for over 80 years.

THE GREATEST MIRACLE IN THE WORLD by Og Mandino. Approximate price $35. This book has sold over five million copies. When you read it, you will know why.

MAKING MONEY MADE SIMPLE by Noel Whittaker. Approximate price $25. This covers the principles of finance, tax and investment and follows naturally from this book.

THE 7 HABITS OF HIGHLY EFFECTIVE PEOPLE by Stephen Covey. Approximate price $30. This is a great work on goal setting on how to get ahead.

THINK AND GROW RICH by Napoleon Hill. Approximate price $20. This book has changed tens of thousands of lives. It may change yours too.

UNIVERSITY OF SUCCESS by Og Mandino. Approximate price $42. This book contains excerpts from many of the leading success books that have been written over time. It will help you choose which authors you would like to read next.

HOW TO WIN FRIENDS AND INFLUENCE PEOPLE by Dale Carnegie. Approximate price $25. One of the greatest books on human relations ever published.

INFLUENCE: THE PSYCHOLOGY OF PERSUASION by Robert Cialdini. Approximate price $33. This is the definitive book on the sales process and is a must for anybody interested in sales.

You will notice the total cost of all the books listed above is less then $250. Just think about it. If you invested only $5 a week for one year, you'd be able to buy each of these books. You would then have one of the best success libraries in the country containing information that may be worth millions of dollars to you. It is also an asset that won't wear out and one that will bring you increasing joy as the years pass.

Many of the people who write to me say "Your books have changed my life but I wish I had read this material 30 years ago". You have a head start because the material is ready and waiting for you. All you have to do is read it.

To keep up to date
with the latest financial news, visit Noel's website at:

www.noelwhittaker.com.au

Where you can...
- subscribe to Noel's regular e-newsletter
- download his recent columns
- buy more of Noel's products
- ask questions relating to your financial situation, and
- much more.

Congratulations!

If you are ready to take the next step of your financial journey, order the 20th Anniversary Edition of *Making Money Made Simple.*

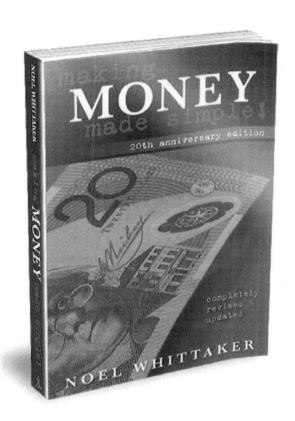

This is the most successful and influential of all Noel's books. *Making Money Made Simple* smashed sales records and sold over a million copies around the world. It stayed on the best-sellers list for a record nine years, and was voted in the Top 100 of the Most Influential Books of the 20th Century. After a complete revamp in

2009, *Making Money Made Simple* is back better than ever to teach you the essentials of money, investment, borrowing and personal finance in a way that only Noel knows how.

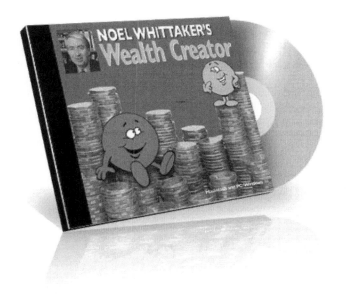

Most of the calculations in this book have been done with the Noel Whittaker *Wealth Creator* CD-ROM.

The Noel Whittaker *Wealth Creator CD-ROM* is as simple to operate as a Fisher Price toy and includes three sections.

The first is "The Educators" that graphically illustrates money principles such as compound interest and the Rule of 72. It also has a module "Dollar Cost Averaging" that enables you to choose any starting month after January 1980 and enter a hypothetical monthly investment figure. All you have to do is enter any finishing month and it will calculate how much you would have had if your investment matched the All Ordinaries Accumulation Index. This model updates itself automatically every month so the information is always right up to date.

The second section "The Calculators" contains six calculators for loans, savings, retirement planning, superannuation and retirement draw-downs. There is also a stock market module that is also updated monthly – this calculator enables you to enter a single lump sum and find out what it would have grown to.

The third section is "The Recorders" that enables you to work out your personal assets and liability statement, personal budget and also maintain a register for insurance purposes.

Full details are atwww.noelwhittaker.com.au

Have a large corporate order?

Email Noel at

noel@noelwhittaker.com.au

and find out about the

special offers for large orders.

BACK COVER MATERIAL

THE IDEAL "STARTER BOOK" FOR YOUNG PEOPLE

UNWRAP THE SECRETS TO A SUCCESSFUL FINANCIAL FUTURE

This book is much more than a simple introduction to finance; it also focuses on building the skills to make money in this rapidly changing world.

CONTENTS INCLUDE

The magic formula • Budgeting • Principles of wealth • Building a better you • Credit cards • The universal laws • The miracle of compound interest • Give it a try! • Staying away from trouble • Changing your self-image • How to earn more money • Why "most people" fail • Investments for young people • Setting goals • Making interest work for you • Re-framing your life • The law of Sowing and Reaping • Going into business • Avoiding the debt trap • Managing your money • Understanding failure • Finding your inner power

NOEL WHITTAKER
FCPA FAIM FTIA AFPA

Noel Whittaker reaches over seven million people each week through his columns in major Australian newspapers, such as *The Sydney Morning Herald,* Melbourne's *The Age,* Perth's *The Sunday Times* and Brisbane's *The Sunday Mail,* and his regular appearances on television and radio.

His other bestselling books include *Making Money Made Simple, More Money with Noel Whittaker, Living Well in Retirement, Golden Rules of Wealth* and Australasia's first Personal Financial Planning CD-ROM—*The Noel Whittaker Wealth Creator.*

JAMES WHITTAKER
BA BBUS(MGT) DIPFS(FP) AMAMI

James Whittaker has a diverse background in marketing, writing, finance, real estate and business management. James is currently the Business Development Manager for Whittaker Macnaught, where he has worked since 2003. Although he has worked closely with Noel on several other projects, this is his first book as co-author.

274

Books For ALL Kinds of Readers

At ReadHowYouWant we understand that one size does not fit all types of readers. Our innovative, patent pending technology allows us to design new formats to make reading easier and more enjoyable for you. This helps improve your speed of reading and your comprehension. Our EasyRead printed books have been optimized to improve word recognition, ease eye tracking by adjusting word and line spacing as well as minimizing hyphenation. Our EasyRead SuperLarge editions have been developed to make reading easier and more accessible for vision-impaired readers. We offer Braille and DAISY formats of our books and all popular E-Book formats.

We are continually introducing new formats based upon research and reader preferences. Visit our web-site to see all of our formats and learn how you can Personalize our books for yourself or as gifts. Sign up to Become A (RHYW) Registered Reader.

www.readhowyouwant.com

Printed in Great Britain
by Amazon.co.uk, Ltd.,
Marston Gate.